AA

F...

BELGIUM & THE NETHERLANDS

Contents

Map pages	II
Map symbols	III
Route planner	IV
Distance chart	1
Road atlas	2-44
Index and city environs plans	45-60

Amsterdam	45	Luxembourg	52
Brussel/Bruxelles	47	Paris	54-55

6th edition January 2008

© Automobile Association Developments Limited 2008.

Original edition printed 1996.

 This product includes mapping data licensed from Ordnance Survey® with the permission of the Controller of Her Majesty's Stationery Office. © Crown copyright 2008. All rights reserved. Licence number 100021153.

All rights reserved. No part of this publication may be reproduced, stored in a retrieval system, or transmitted in any form or by any means – electronic, mechanical, photocopying, recording or otherwise – unless the permission of the publisher has been given beforehand.

Published by AA Publishing (a trading name of Automobile Association Developments Limited, whose registered office is Fanum House, Basing View, Basingstoke, Hampshire RG21 4EA, UK. Registered number 1878835).

Cartography edited, designed and produced by the Mapping Services Department of The Automobile Association. This atlas has been compiled and produced from the Automaps database utilising electronic and computer technology (A03556).

ISBN-13: 978 0 7495 5604 4

A CIP catalogue for this book is available from The British Library.

Printed in Italy by Printer Trento srl on F.S.C. accredited paper.
Paper: Gardamatt 100gsm

The contents of this atlas are believed to be correct at the time of the latest revision. However, the publishers cannot be held responsible for loss occasioned to any person acting or refraining from action as a result of any material in this atlas, nor for any errors, omissions or changes in such material. This does not affect your statutory rights. The publishers would welcome information to correct any errors or omissions and to keep this atlas up to date. Please write to the The atlas editor, AA Publishing, Fanum House, Basing View, Basingstoke, Hampshire RG21 4EA, UK.

E-mail: *roadatlasfeedback@theaa.com*

Mixed Sources

Product group from well-managed forests and other controlled sources
www.fsc.org Cert no. CQ-COC-000012
© 1996 Forest Stewardship Council

FSC

Map pages

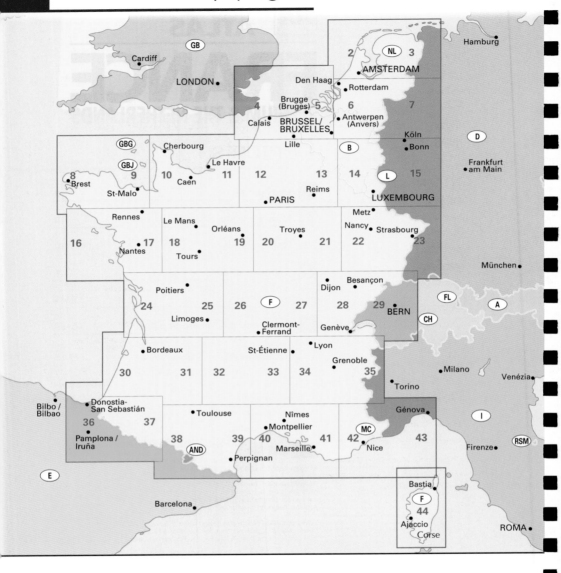

A Austria	**F** France	**GBG** Guernsey
AND Andorra	**FL** Liechtenstein	**GBJ** Jersey
B Belgium	**GB** United Kingdom of Great Britain and Northern Ireland	**I** Italy
CH Switzerland		**L** Luxembourg
D Germany		**MC** Monaco
E Spain		

NL The Netherlands
RSM San Marino

Map symbols

Toll-free motorways

A15 / E31	Dual carriageway with road numbers
	Single carriageway
12	Interchange
12	Restricted interchange
S	Service area
2009	Under construction (opening year)

Toll motorways

A6 / E15	Dual carriageway with road numbers
	Single carriageway
12	Interchange
12	Restricted interchange
S	Service area
2009	Under construction (opening year)

National roads

N10	Dual carriageway with road number
	Single carriageway

Regional roads

N10	Dual carriageway with road number
	Single carriageway

Local roads

N42	Dual carriageway with road number
	Single carriageway
D2	Minor road with road number

 Page overlap and number

Symbols

E15 E50	European international network numbers
	Motorway in tunnel
	Road in tunnel
2009	Road under construction (opening year)
	Toll point
63 23	Distances in kilometres
	Gradient 14% and over
	Gradient 6%-13%
Col de la Croix de Fer 2067 11-5	Mountain pass with closure period
	Panoramic routes
Bastia	Ferry route with car transportation
	Railway and tunnel
	National park, natural reserve
⊕	International Airport
	Religious building; Castle
	Monument; Ruins, archaeological area
	Viewpoint (180° or 360°)
Ω *	Cave; Natural curiosity
★	Other curiosity
PARIS	Town or place of great tourist interest
Carnac	Interesting town or place
St-Lô	Other tourist town or place
Vars	Ski resort, mountain tourist resort

Boundaries

	International
	Internal

Scale

1 : 1 000 000

10 kilometres : 1 centimetre

16 miles : 1 inch

Route planner

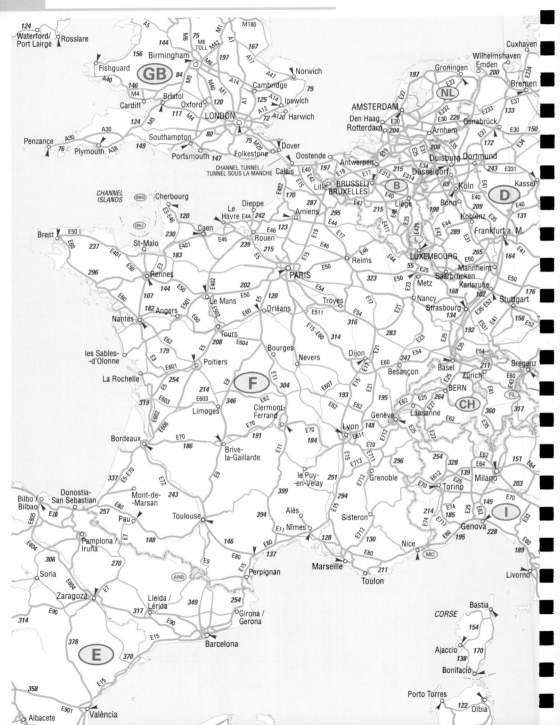

Distance chart

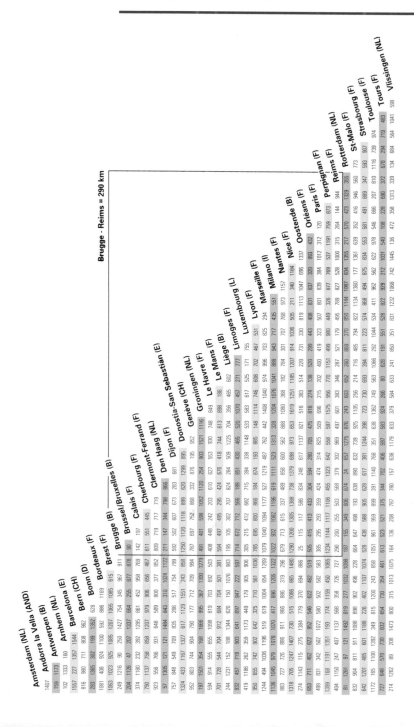

Brugge - Reims = 290 km

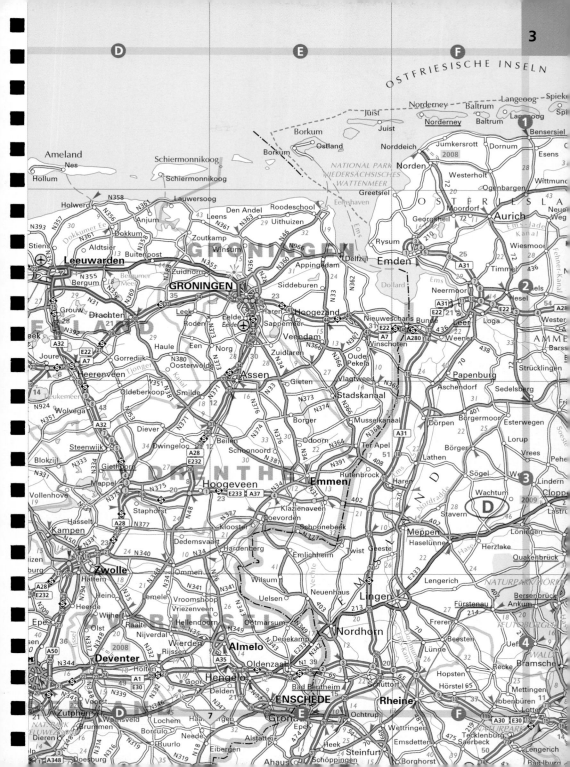

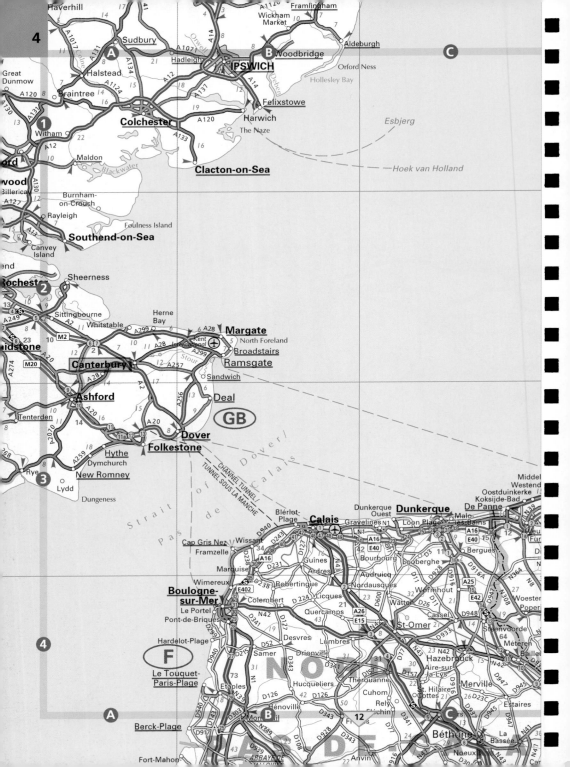

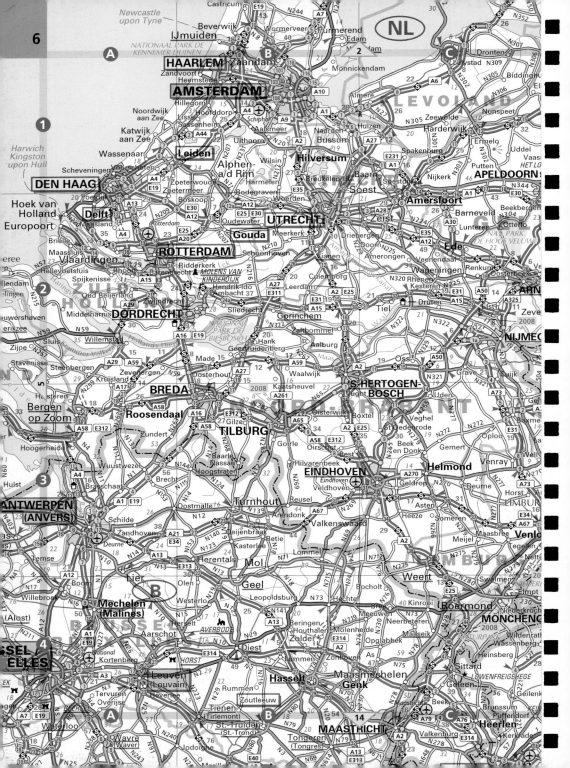

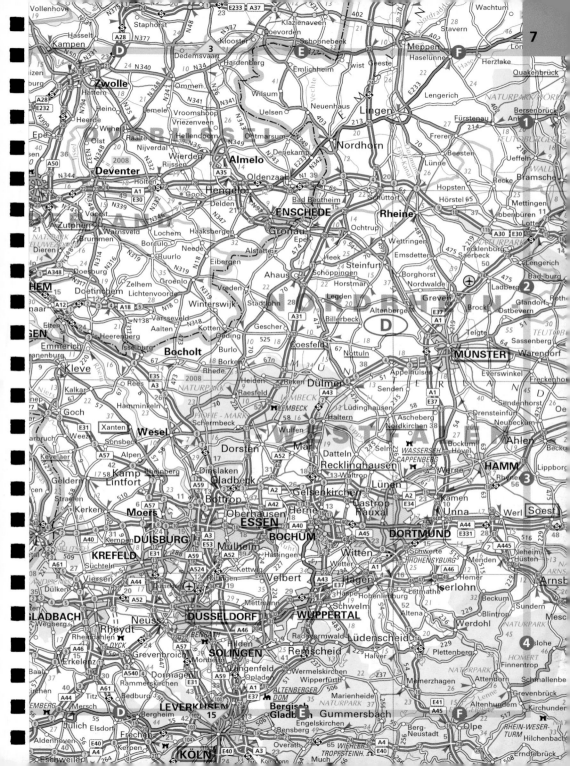

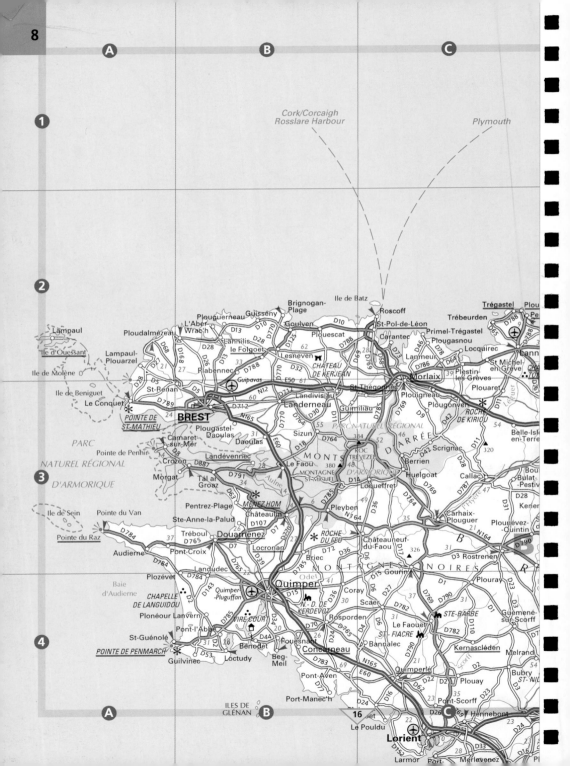

A   B   C

1

Cork/Corcaigh
Rosslare Harbour   Plymouth

2

Lampaul
Île d'Ouessant

Île de Molène

Île de Beniguet
Le Conquet

POINTE DE
ST-MATHIEU

PARC

NATUREL RÉGIONAL

3 D'ARMORIQUE

Île de Sein   Pointe du Van

Pointe du Raz

Audierne

Baie
d'Audierne

CHAPELLE
DE LANGUIDOU

Plonéour Lanvern

Pont-l'Abbé

4 POINTE DE PENMARCH

St-Guénolé
Guilvinec   Loctudy   Bénodet
Beg-
Meil

ÎLES DE
GLÉNAN

Ploudalmézeau
L'Aber-
Wrach
Lannilis
le Folgoët
Plabennec

St-Renan

BREST

Plougastel-
Daoulas   Daoulas

Camaret-
sur-Mer
Crozon
Landévennec
Morgat   Tal ar
Groaz

Pentrez-Plage
Ste-Anne-la-Palud
Tréboul   Châteaulin
Douarnenez
Pont-Croix   Locronan

Landudec
Plozévet

Quimper-
Pluguffan
Quimper

VIRE COURT

Plouguerneau   Guissény

Goulven
Plouescat

Lesneven

CHÂTEAU
DE KERJEAN

Guipavas

Landivisiau
Landerneau

Sizun

Le Faou
MONTAGNE
ST-MICHEL

MENEZ HOM

D107

ROCHE
DU FEU

Briec

MONTS
D'ARRÉE
ROC
TRÉVEZEL
D'ARMORIQUE

Pleyben

Châteauneuf-
du-Faou

Coray
Scaër
Rosporden

N.-D. DE
KERDEVOT

Gourin

Plouray

Ste-Anne-la-Palud

Brignogan-
Plage   Île de Batz
Roscoff
St-Pol-de-Léon
Cérantec

Primel-Trégastel
Plougasnou
Lanmeur
Locquirec

St Michel-
en-Grève
Morlaix
Plestin-
les-Grèves
Plouaret
Plouigneau
Plougonven
ROCHE
DE KIRIOU
Scrignac
Berrien
Huelgoat
Loqueffret

D764

Callac

Carhaix-
Plouguer

Le Faouet
ST-FIACRE
Bannalec

STE-BARBE

Kernascléden

Trégastel
Trébeurden

Lann

St Michel-

Belle-Isle-
en-Terre

Bou
Bulat-
Pestiv

Kerien

D28

Plounévez-
Quintin

B

Guémené-
sur-Scorff

Melrand

Bubry
ST-NIC

Plourin

Pont-Aven

Concarneau
Fouesnant

Quimperlé
Plouay

Pont-Scorff
Hennebont
Port-Manec'h
Le Pouldu
Lorient
Larmor
Merlevenez

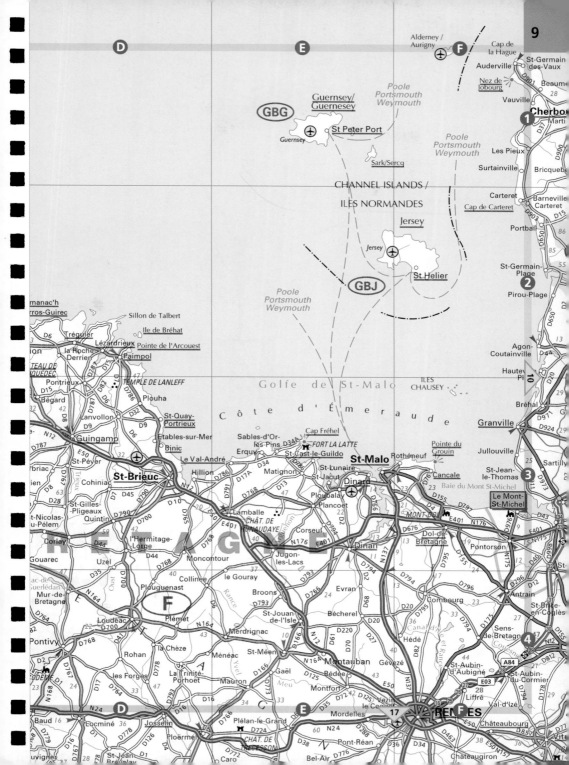

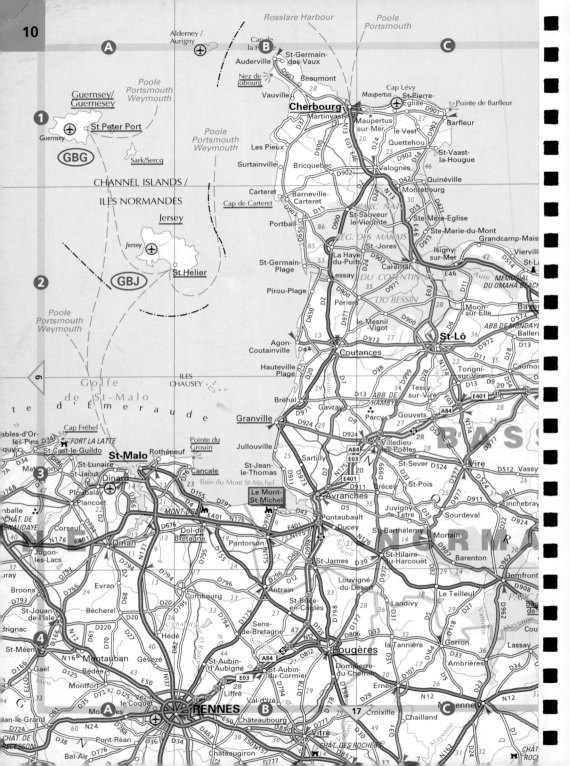

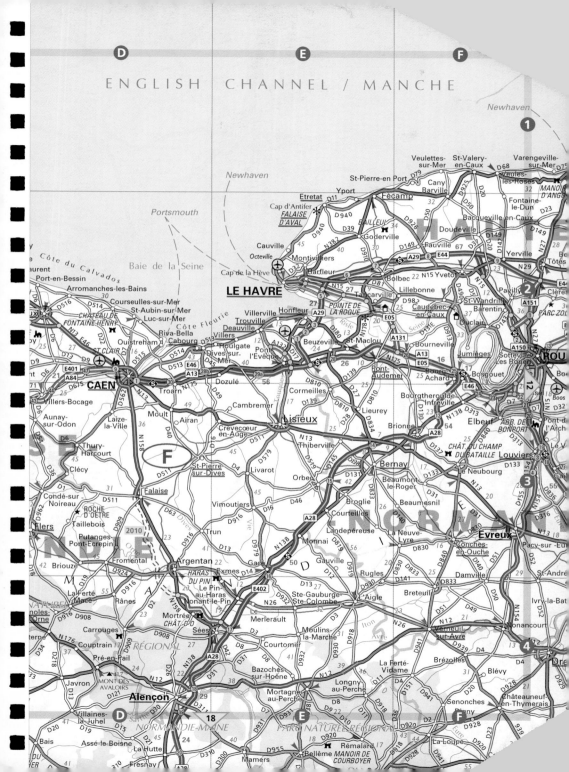

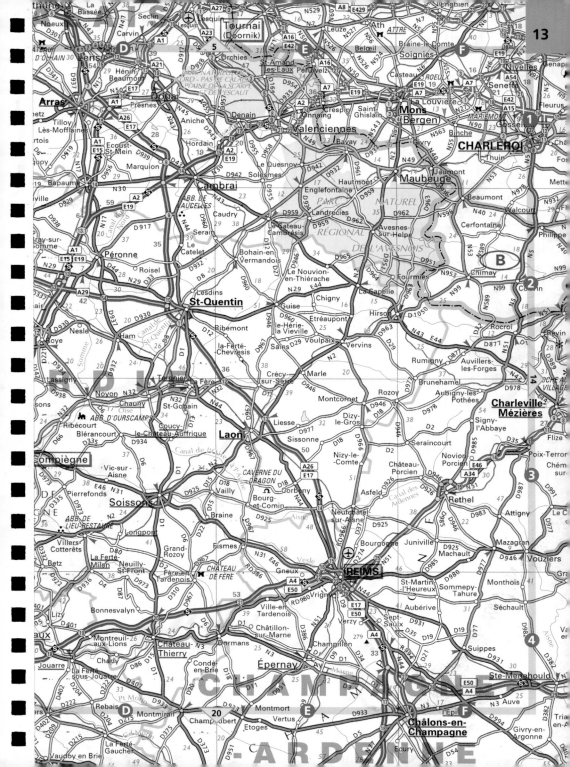

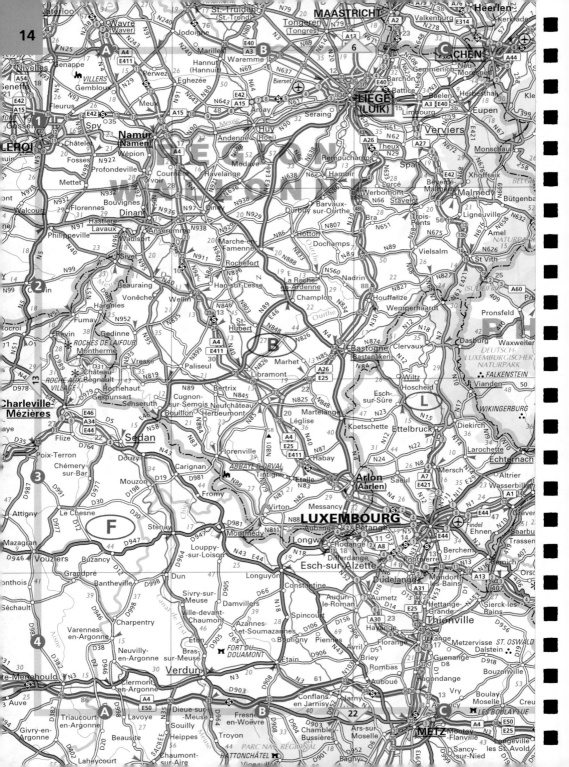

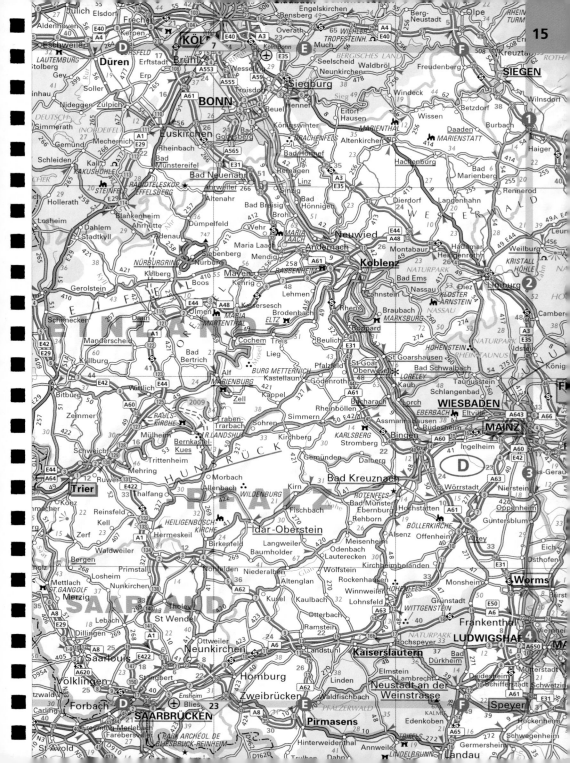

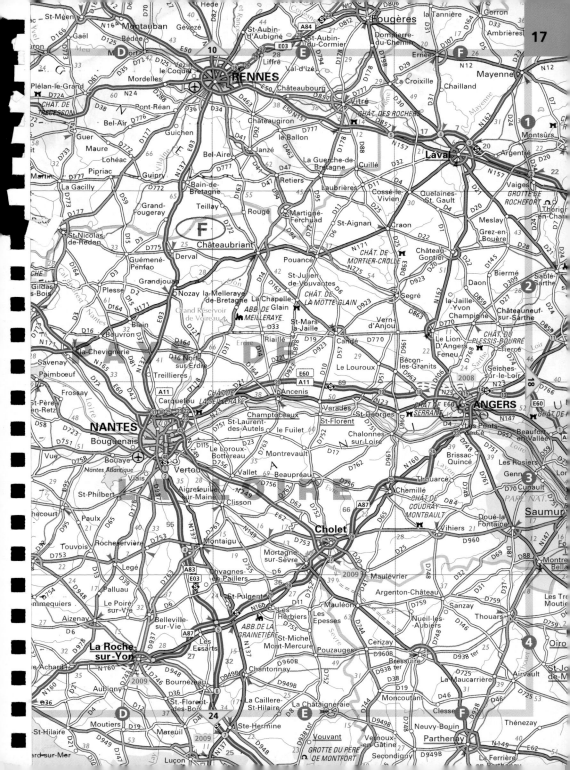

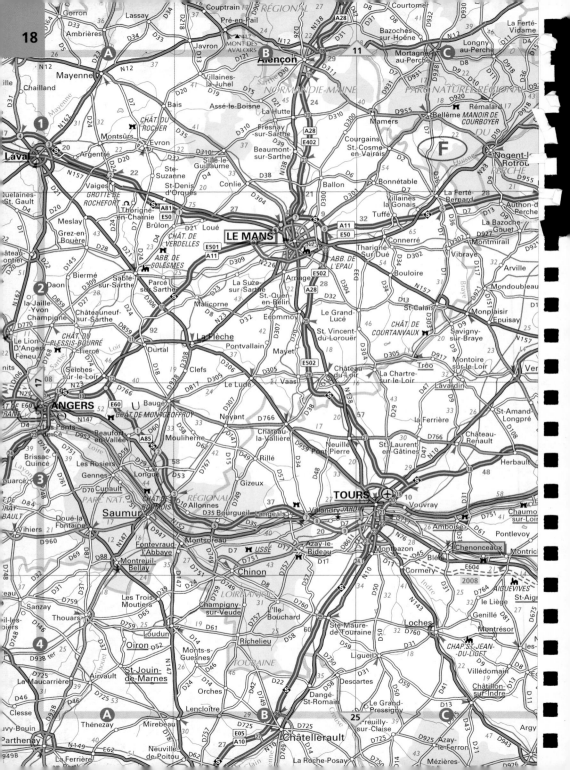

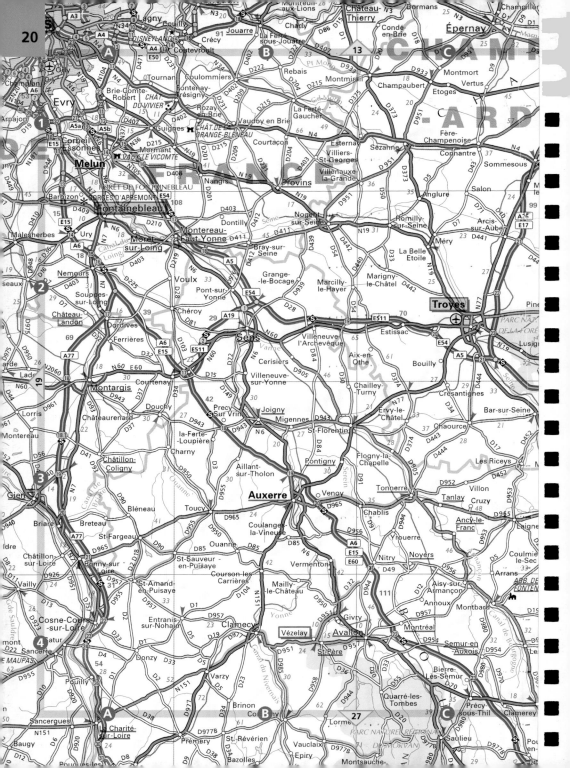

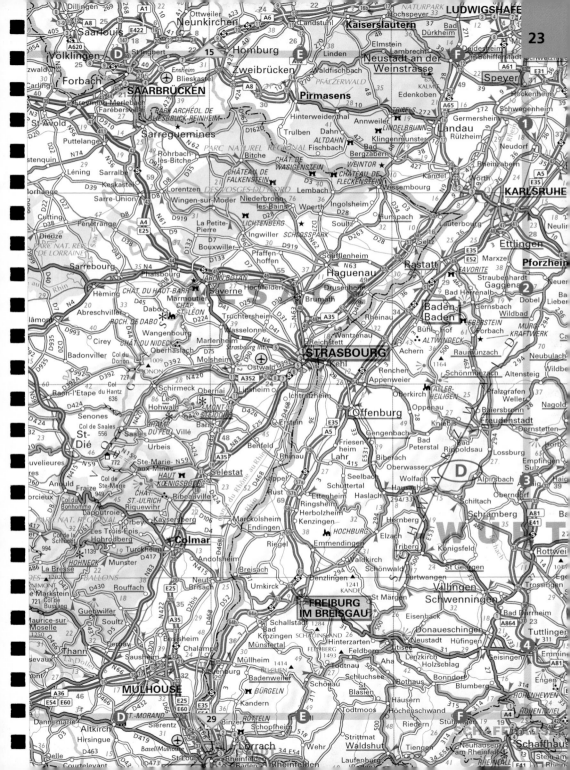

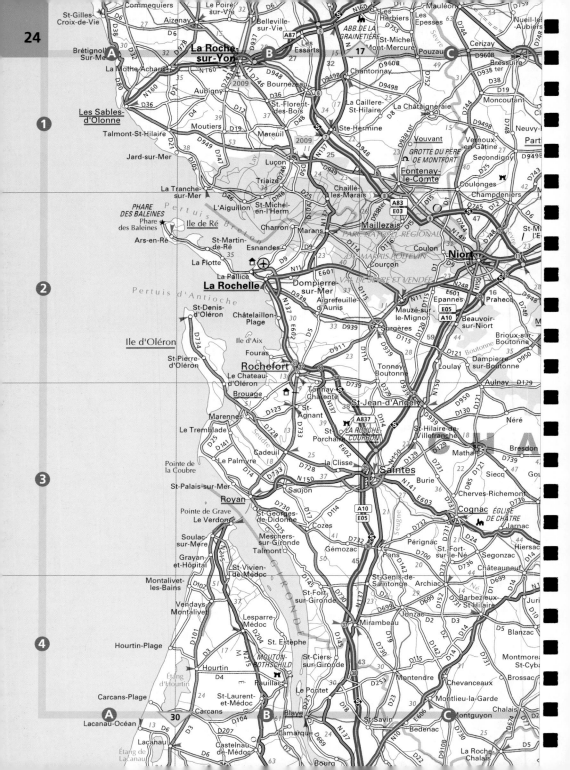

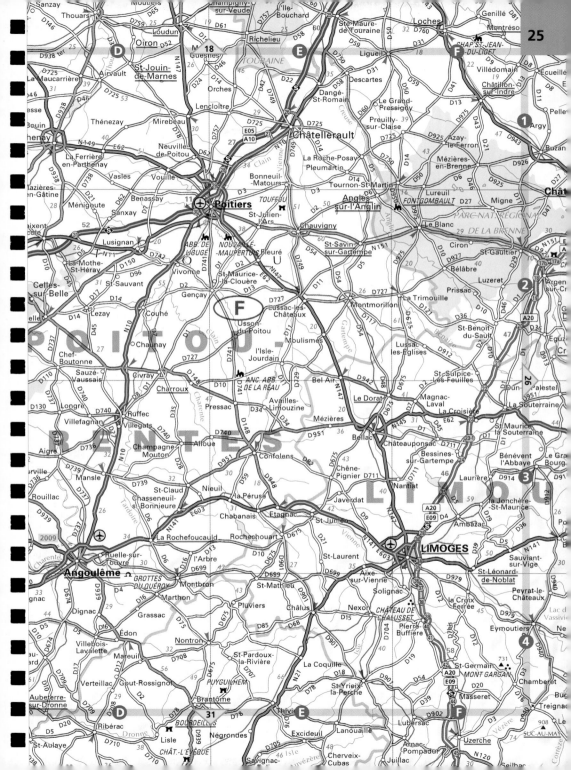

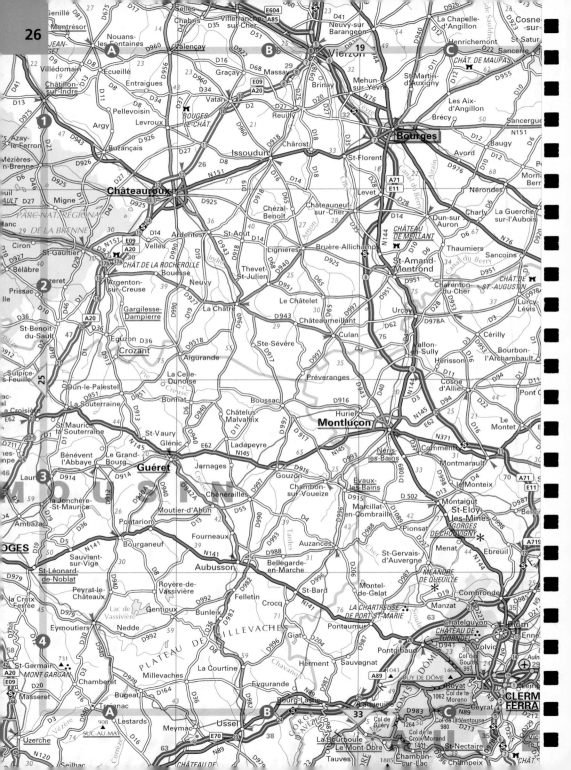

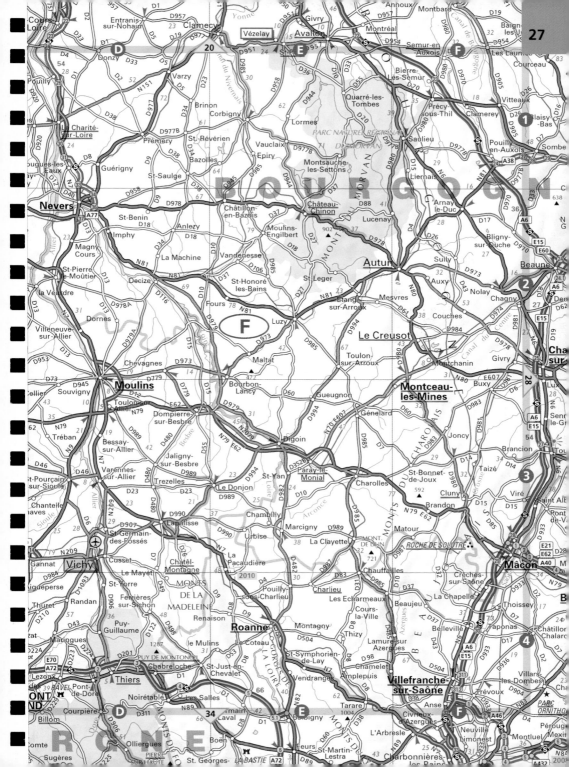

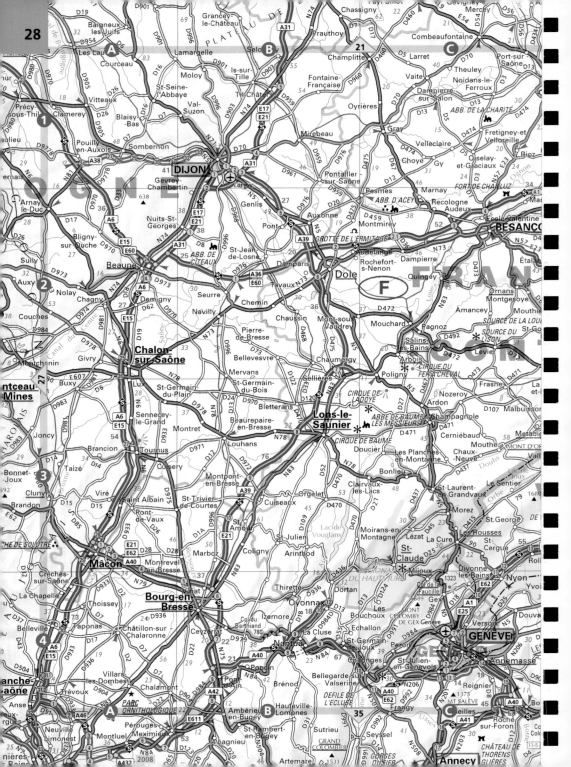

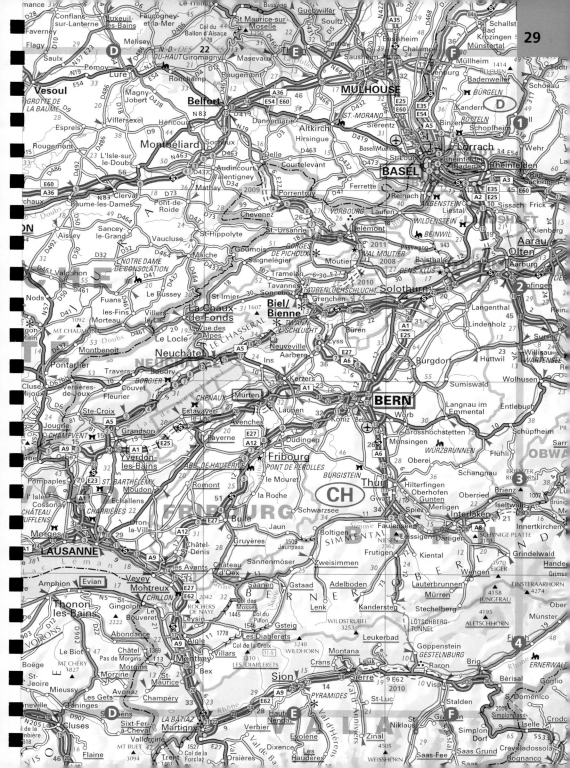

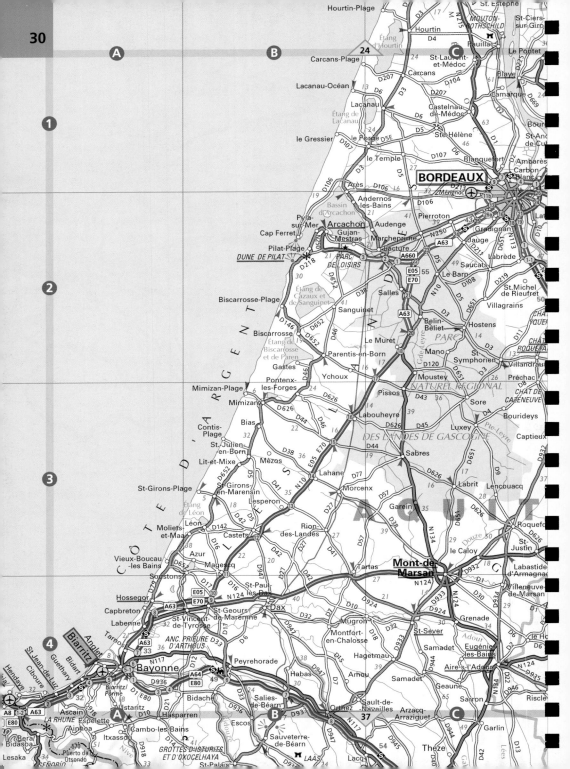

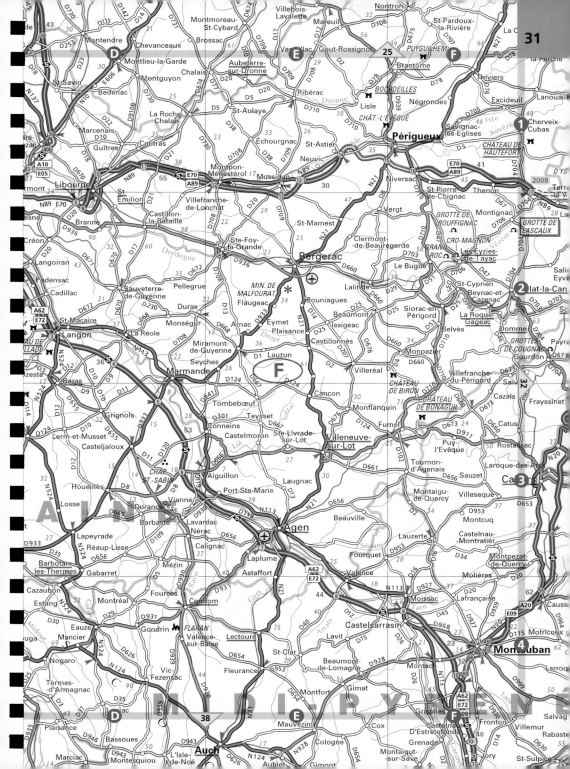

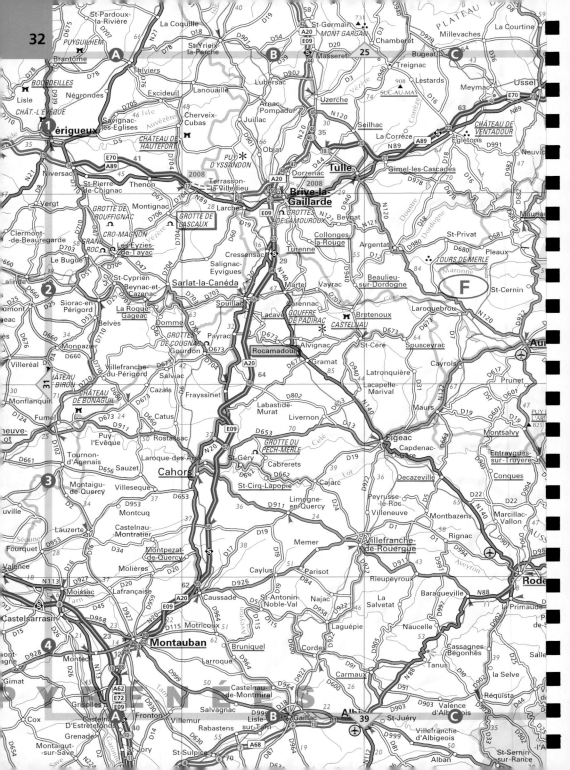

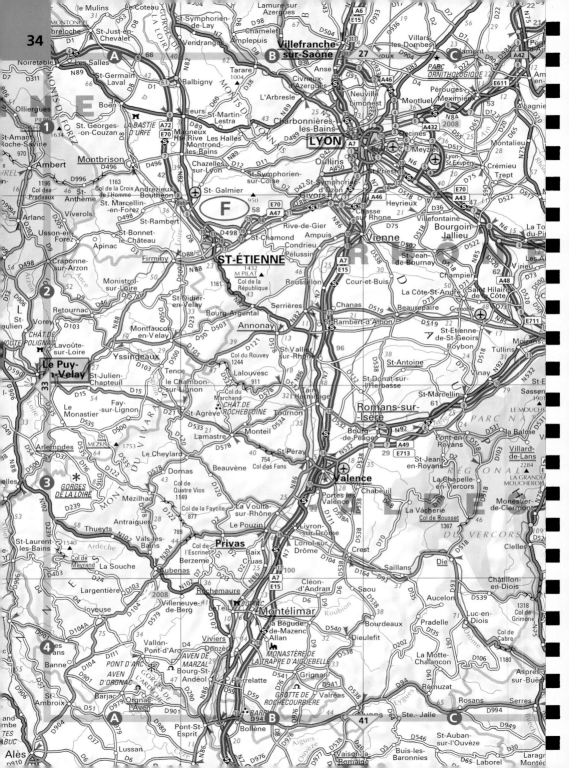

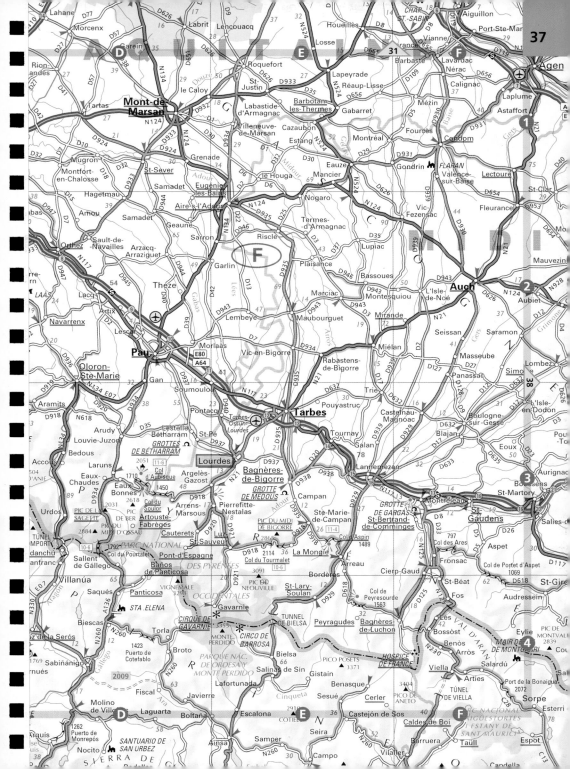

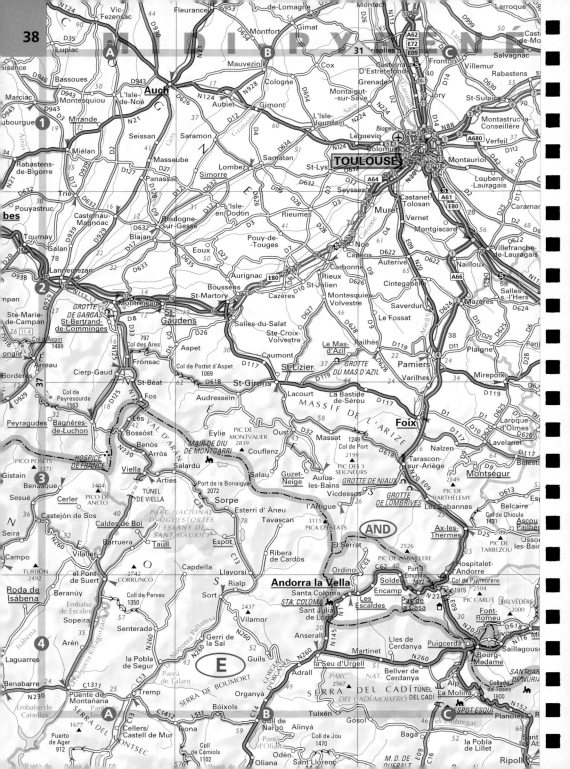

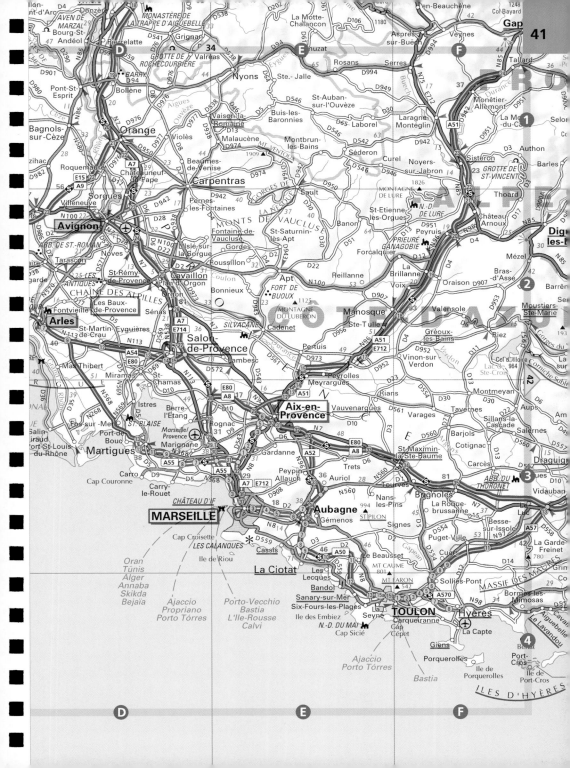

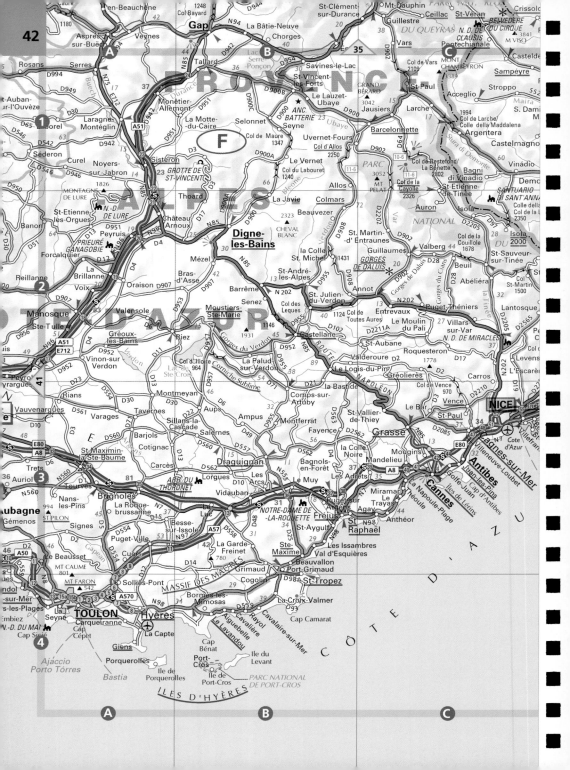

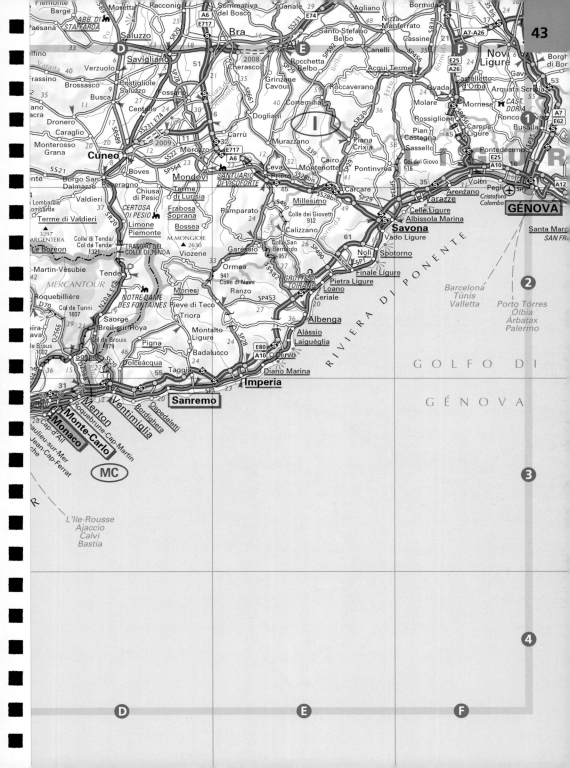

How to use the index

The index lists the place names, tourist sites, main tunnels and passes contained in the atlas, followed by the abbreviation of the country name to which they belong. All names contained in two adjoining pages are referenced to the even page number.

A

Aalburg [NL] 6 B2
Aalsmeer [NL] 2 B4
Aalst (Alost) [B] 4 E4
Aalten [NL] 6 D2
Aalter [B] 4 E3
Aarschot [B] 6 B4
Abbaye d'Orval [B] 14 B3
Abbeville [F] 12 B1
Abéliéra [F] 42 C2
Ablis [F] 18 E1
Abondance [F] 28 D4
Abreschviller [F] 22 D2
Abriès [F] 34 F4
Accous [F] 36 D3

Acey, Abbaye d'– [F] 28 C2
Acheux-en-Amiénois [F] 12 C1
Acqua Doria [F] 44 A3
Afsluitdijk [NL] 2 C2
Agay [F] 42 C3
Agde [F] 38 F3
Agen [F] 30 E3
Agon-Coutainville [F] 10 B2
Aignay-le-Duc [F] 20 D4
Aigre [F] 24 D3
Aigrefeuille-d'Aunis [F] 24 B2
Aigrefeuille-sur-Maine [F] 16 D3
Aiguebelle [F] 34 E2
Aiguebelle [F] 42 B4
Aigueperse [F] 26 C4
Aigues-Mortes [F] 40 C2
Aigues-Vives [F] 38 E2

Aiguevives [F] 18 C4
Aiguilles [F] 34 E4
Aigurande [F] 26 B2
Ailefroide [F] 34 E3
Aillant-sur-Tholon [F] 20 B3
Aime [F] 34 E2
Ainhoa [F] 36 B2
Airaines [F] 12 B2
Airan [F] 10 D3
Aire [F] 4 C4
Aire-sur-l'Adour [F] 30 C4
Airvault [F] 16 F4
Aisey-sur-Seine [F] 20 D3
Aïssey [F] 28 D2
Aisy-sur-Armançon [F] 20 C4
Aix-en-Othe [F] 20 C2
Aix-en-Provence [F] 40 E3
Aixe-sur-Vienne [F] 24 E3
Aix-les-Bains [F] 34 D2

Aizenay [F] 16 D4
Ajaccio [F] 44 A3
Alban [F] 38 E1
Albens [F] 34 D1
Albert [F] 12 C2
Albertacce [F] 44 B2
Albertville [F] 34 E2
Albi [F] 38 D1
Albier Montrond [F] 34 E3
Albo [F] 44 C1
Aldtsier [NL] 2 D2
Alençon [F] 10 D4
Aléria [F] 44 C3
Aléria [F] 44 C3
Algajola [F] 44 B2
Alkmaar [NL] 2 B3
Allaines [F] 18 E2
Allainville [F] 18 E1
Allan [F] 34 B4
Allanche [F] 32 D2
Allauch [F] 40 E3
Allemont [F] 34 D3
Alleuze, Château d'– [F] 32 D2
Allevard [F] 34 D2
Allonnes [F] 18 B3
Allos [F] 42 B1

Alloue [F] 24 E3
Almelo [NL] 2 E4
Almere [NL] 2 C4
Alost (Aalst) [B] 4 E4
Alpe du Grand Serre [F] 34 D3
Alphen-aan den Rijn [NL] 2 B4
Altkirch [F] 28 E1
Altrier [L] 14 C3
Alvignac [F] 32 B2
Alzon [F] 40 B1
Alzonne [F] 38 D2
Amance [F] 20 F4
Amancey [F] 28 C2
Amay [B] 14 B1
Ambarès [F] 30 D1
Ambazac [F] 24 F3
Ambérieu-en-Bugey [F] 34 C1
Ambert [F] 32 F1
Amboise [F] 18 C3
Ambrières [F] 10 C4
Amel [B] 14 C2
Amélie-les-Bains [F] 38 D4
Amerongen [NL] 6 C2
Amersfoort [NL] 2 C4
Amiens [F] 12 C2
Amou [F] 30 B4

Amphion [F] 28 D4
Amplepuis [F] 26 E4
Ampuis [F] 34 B2
Ampus [F] 42 B3
Amsterdam [NL] 2 B3
Anc. Batterie [F] 42 B1
Ancenis [F] 16 E3
Ancerville [F] 20 E2
Ancy–le–Franc [F] 20 C3
Andelot [F] 20 E3
Andenne [B] 14 B1
Andernos–les–Bains [F] 30 B2
Andijk [NL] 2 C3
Andolsheim [F] 22 D3
Andrézieux–Bouthéon [F]
  34 A2
Anduze [F] 40 C1
Anet [F] 12 A4
Angers [F] 16 F3
Angerville [F] 18 E2
Angles–sur–l'Anglin [F] 24 E2
Anglet [F] 30 A4
Anglure [F] 20 C2
Ango, Manoir d'– [F] 12 A1
Angoulême [F] 24 D3
Aniane [F] 40 B2
Aniche [F] 12 D1
Anjum [NL] 2 D2
Anlezy [F] 26 D2
Anna Paulowna [NL] 2 B2
Annecy [F] 34 E1
Annemasse [F] 28 C4
Annonay [F] 34 B2
Annot [F] 42 B2
Annoux [F] 20 C4
Anse [F] 26 F4
Anseremme [B] 14 A2
Anthéor [F] 42 C3
Antibes [F] 42 C3
Antraigues [F] 34 A3
Antrain [F] 8 F4
Antwerpen (Anvers) [B] 4 F3
Anvers (Antwerpen) [B] 4 F3
Apchon [F] 32 D2
Apeldoorn [NL] 2 D4
Apinac [F] 32 F2
Apothicairerie, Grotte de l'– [F]
  16 B2
Appingedam [NL] 2 E2
Apremont, Gorges d'– [F]
  18 F2
Apt [F] 40 E2
Aramits [F] 36 D3
Arbois [F] 28 C2
Arc, Pont d'– [F] 34 A4
Arcachon [F] 30 B2
Arcen [NL] 6 D3
Arc–en–Barrois [F] 20 D3
Arches [F] 22 C3
Archiac [F] 24 C4
Arcis–sur–Aube [F] 20 C2
Ardentes [F] 26 B2
Ardon [F] 28 C3
Ardres [F] 4 B4
Areches–Beaufort [F] 34 E2
Arendonk [B] 6 B3
Arès [F] 30 B2
Argancy [F] 14 C4
Argelès–Gazost [F] 36 E3
Argelès–Plage [F] 38 E4
Argelès–sur–Mer [F] 38 E4
Argentan [F] 10 D3
Argentat [F] 32 C2
Argentella [F] 44 B2
Argentière [F] 34 F1
Argenton–Château [F] 16 F4
Argenton–sur–Creuse [F]
  26 A2
Argentré [F] 16 F1
Argent–sur–Sauldre [F] 18 E3
Argy [F] 26 A1
Arinthod [F] 28 B3

Arlanc [F] 32 F2
Arlempdes [F] 32 F3
Arles [F] 40 D2
Arles–sur–Tech [F] 38 D4
Arlon (Aarlen) [B] 14 B3
Armentières [F] 4 D4
Arnac [F] 30 E2
Arnac–Pompadur [F] 32 B1
Arnage [F] 18 B2
Arnay–le–Duc [F] 26 F2
Arnhem [NL] 6 C2
Arnould [F] 22 D3
Arpajon [F] 18 E1
Arracourt [F] 22 C2
Arrans [F] 20 C3–4
Arras [F] 12 D1
Arreau [F] 36 E3
Arrens–Marsous [F] 36 D3
Arromanches–les–Bains [F]
  10 D2
Arronville [F] 12 B3
Ars–en–Ré [F] 24 A2
Ars–sur–Moselle [F] 22 C1
Arsy [F] 12 C3
Artemare [F] 34 D1
Artenay [F] 18 E2
Arthous, Ancient Prieure d'– [F]
  30 B4
Artix [F] 36 D2
Artouste–Fabrèges [F] 36 D3
Arudy [F] 36 D3
Arvieux [F] 34 E4
Arville [F] 18 C2
Arzacq–Arraziguet [F] 36 D2
Ascain [F] 30 A4
Asco [F] 44 B2
Ascou–Pailhères [F] 38 CD3
Asfeld [F] 12 E3
Aspet [F] 36 F3
Aspres–sur–Buëch [F] 34 D4
Assé–le–Boisne [F] 18 B1
Assen [NL] 2 E2
Astaffort [F] 30 E4
Asten [NL] 6 C3
Attigny [F] 12 F3
Aubagne [F] 40 E3
Aubange [B] 14 B3
Aubenas [F] 34 A3
Aubérive [F] 12 F4
Auberive [F] 20 D3
Auberterre–sur–Dronne [F]
  30 E1
Aubiet [F] 38 B1
Aubigny [F] 16 D4
Aubigny–les–Pothées [F]
  12 F3
Aubigny–sur–Nère [F] 18 E3
Aboué [F] 14 C4
Aubrac [F] 32 D3
Aubusson [F] 26 B3
Aucelon [F] 34 C4
Auch [F] 36 F2
Audelange [F] 28 B2
Audenge [F] 30 C2
Auderville [F] 8 F1
Audeux [F] 28 C2
Audierne [F] 8 A3
Audincourt [F] 28 E1
Audressein [F] 38 B3
Audun–le–Roman [F] 14 C4
Aulène [F] 44 B3
Aulnay [F] 24 C3
Ault [F] 12 B1
Aulus–les–Bains [F] 38 B3
Aumale [F] 12 B2
Aumetz [F] 14 C4
Aumont–Aubrac [F] 32 E3
Aunay–sur–Odon [F] 10 D3
Auneau [F] 18 E1
Auneuil [F] 12 B3
Aups [F] 40 F3
Auray [F] 16 B1

Aurignac [F] 38 B2
Aurillac [F] 32 C2
Auriol [F] 40 E3
Auron [F] 42 C2
Auterive [F] 38 C2
Authon [F] 42 B1
Authon–du–Perche [F] 18 C2
Autun [F] 26 F2
Auve [F] 12 F4
Auvers–s–Oise [F] 12 B3
Auvillers–les–Forges [F] 12 F2
Auxerre [F] 20 B3
Auxy [F] 26 F2
Auxi–le–Château [F] 12 C1
Auxonne [F] 28 B2
Auzances [F] 26 B3
Auzon [F] 32 E2
Availles–Limouzine [F] 24 E3
Aval, Falaise d'– [F] 10 E2
Avallon [F] 20 C4
Aven Armand [F] 32 E4
Aven de Marzal [F] 34 A4
Aven d'Orgnac [F] 34 A4
Avène [F] 38 F1–2
Averbode [B] 6 B4
Avesnes–le–Comte [F] 12 C1
Avesnes–sur–Helpe [F] 12 E2
Avignon [F] 40 D2
Avord [F] 26 C1
Avoriaz [F] 28 D4
Avranches [F] 10 B3
Avril [F] 14 C4
Axat [F] 38 D3
Axel [NL] 4 E3
Ax–les–Thermes [F] 38 C3
Ay [F] 12 E4
Azannes–et–Soumazannes [F]
  14 B4
Azay–le–Ferron [F] 24 F1
Azay–le–Rideau [F] 18 B3
Azur [F] 30 B3

B

Baarle Nassau [NL] 6 B3
Baarn [NL] 2 C4
Baccarat [F] 22 C2
Bacqueville–en–Caux [F]
  12 A2
Badonviller [F] 22 D2
Baelen [B] 14 C1
Bagnères–de–Bigorre [F] 36 E3
Bagnères–de–Luchon [F]
  36 F4
Bagnoles–de–l'Orne [F] 10 D4
Bagnols–en–Forêt [F] 42 B3
Bagnols–les–Bains [F] 32 E3
Bagnols–sur–Cèze [F] 40 D1
Baigneux–les–Juifs [F] 20 D4
Bailleul [F] 4 C4
Bailleul [F] 10 E2
Bain–de–Bretagne [F] 16 D1
Bains–les–Bains [F] 22 C3
Bais [F] 18 A1
Baix [F] 34 B3
Baixas [F] 38 E4
Balbigny [F] 34 A1
Baleines, Phare des– [F] 24 A2
Balleroy [F] 10 C2
Ballon [F] 18 B1
Bandol [F] 40 E4
Bangor [F] 16 B2
Bannalec [F] 8 C4
Banne [F] 32 A4
Banon [F] 40 E2
Bantheville [F] 14 A4
Banyuls–sur–Mer [F] 38 E4

Bapaume [F] 12 D1
Baraqueville [F] 32 C4
Barbaste [F] 30 D3
Barbezieux–St–Hilaire [F]
  24 C4
Barbizon [F] 18 F2
Barbotan–les–Thermes [F]
  30 D4
Barcelonnette [F] 42 C1
Barchon [B] 14 C1
Barendrecht [NL] 6 A2
Barentin [F] 10 F2
Barenton [F] 10 C3
Barfleur [F] 10 C1
Barjac [F] 34 A4
Barjols [F] 40 F3
Bar–le–Duc [F] 20 E1
Barles [F] 42 B1
Barre–des–Cévennes [F] 32 E4
Barr [F] 22 E3
Barrême [F] 42 B2
Barry [F] 34 B4
Bar–sur–Aube [F] 20 D2
Bar–sur–Seine [F] 20 C3
Barvaux–sur–Ourthe [B] 14 BC2
Bassoues [F] 36 E2
Bastelica [F] 44 B3
Bastia [F] 44 C1
Bastogne (Bastenaken) [B]
  14 B2
Battice [B] 14 C1
Batz–sur–Mer [F] 16 C2
Baud [F] 16 B1
Baugé [F] 18 A3
Baugy [F] 26 C1
Baume, Cirque de– [F] 28 B3
Baume, Grotte de la– [F] 20 F4
Baume–les–Dames [F] 28 D2
Baume–les Messieurs, Abbaye
  de– [F] 28 C3
Bavay [F] 12 E1
Bayard [F] 34 D2
Bayeux [F] 10 D2
Bayon [F] 22 C2
Bayonne [F] 30 A4
Bazas [F] 30 D2
Bazoches–sur–Hoëne [F] 10 E4
Bazolles [F] 26 E1
Beaucaire [F] 40 D2
Beaufort–en–Vallée [F] 18 A3
Beaufort–sur–Doron [F] 34 E2
Beaugency [F] 18 D3
Beaujeu [F] 26 F4
Beaulieu–sur–Dordogne [F]
  32 B2
Beaulieu–sur–Mer [F] 42 C3
Beaumes de Venise [F] 40 D2
Beaumesnil [F] 10 F3
Beaumetz [F] 12 D1
Beaumont [B] 12 F2
Beaumont [F] 10 B1
Beaumont [F] 30 E2
Beaumont–de–Lomagne [F]
  30 E4
Beaumont–le–Roger [F] 10 F3
Beaumont–sur–Sarthe [F]
  18 B1
Beaune [F] 28 A2
Beaune–la–Rolande [F] 18 F2
Beaupréau [F] 16 F3
Beauraing [B] 14 A2
Beauregard, Manoir de– [F]
  18 D4
Beaurepaire [F] 34 C2
Beaurepaire–en–Bresse [F]
  28 B3
Beausite [F] 22 A1
Beauvais [F] 12 B3
Beauvallon [F] 42 B3
Beauvène [F] 34 B3

Beauvezer [F] 42 B2
Beauville [F] 30 E3
Beauvoir–sur–Mer [F] 16 C3
Beauvoir–sur–Niort [F]
  24 C2
Bécherel [F] 8 E4
Bécon–les–Granits [F] 16 F2
Bédarieux [F] 38 F2
Bédée [F] 8 E4
Bedenac [F] 30 D1
Bedous [F] 36 D3
Beek [NL] 6 C4
Beek en Donk [NL] 6 C3
Bégard [F] 8 D3
Beg–Meil [F] 8 B4
Beilen [NL] 2 E3
Belâbre [F] 24 F2
Bel Air [F] 24 E2
Bel–Aire [F] 16 E1
Belcaire [F] 38 C3
Bélesta [F] 38 C3
Belfort [F] 22 C4
Belgodère [F] 44 B2
Belin–Béliet [F] 30 C2
Bellac [F] 24 E3
Bellegarde [F] 40 C2
Bellegarde–en–Marche [F]
  26 B3
Bellegarde–sur–Valserine [F]
  28 C4
Belle–Isle–en–Terre [F] 8 C3
Bellême [F] 18 C1
Bellenaves [F] 26 C3
Bellencombre [F] 12 A2
Bellengreville [F] 12 A1
Bellevesvre [F] 28 B2
Belleville [F] 26 F4
Belleville–sur–Vie [F] 16 D4
Belley [F] 34 D1
Belmont–sur–Rance [F] 38 E1
Beloeil [B] 12 E1
Belvedere Campomoro [F]
  44 B4
Belvedere du Cirque [F]
  34 F4
Belz [F] 16 B1
Benassay [F] 24 D2
Bénévent l'Abbaye [F] 26 A3
Benfeld [F] 22 E3
Bénodet [F] 8 B4
Berchem [L] 14 C3
Bergen [NL] 2 B3
Bergen (Mons) [B] 12 F1
Bergen aan Zee [NL] 2 B3
Bergen op Zoom [NL] 4 F3
Bergerac [F] 30 E2
Bergues [F] 4 C3
Bergum [NL] 2 D2
Beringen [B] 6 B4
Bernaville [F] 12 C1
Bernay [F] 10 E3
Berre–l'Etang [F] 40 D3
Berrien [F] 8 C3
Bertrix [B] 14 B3
Berzeme [F] 34 B3
Besançon [F] 28 C2
Bessan [F] 38 F2
Bessans [F] 34 F3
Bessay–sur–Allier [F] 26 D3
Besse–en–Chandesse [F]
  32 D1
Besse–sur–Issole [F] 40 F3
Bessines–sur–Gartempe [F]
  24 F3
Bétharram, Grottes de– [F]
  36 D3
Betz [F] 12 C3
Beuil [F] 42 C2
Beuzeville [F] 10 E2
Béverdé–Malmedy [B] 14 C1–2
Beverwijk [NL] 2 B3
Beynac–et–Cazenac [F] 30 F2

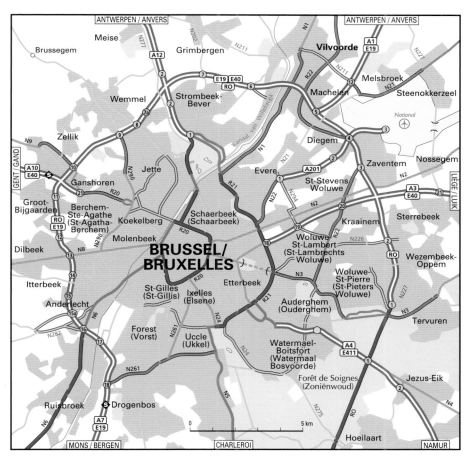

Beynat [F] 32 B2
Béziers [F] 38 F2
Biarritz [F] 30 A4
Bias [F] 30 B3
Bidache [F] 30 B4
Bidart [F] 30 A4
Biddinghuizen [NL] 2 D3
Biermé [F] 18 A2
Bierre–Lès–Semur [F] 20 C4
Billom [F] 32 E1
Binas [F] 18 D2
Binche [B] 12 F1
Binic [F] 8 D3
Biron, Château de– [F] 30 F2
Biscarrosse [F] 30 B2
Biscarrosse–Plage [F] 30 B2
Bitche [F] 22 E1
Blain [F] 16 D2
Blaisy–Bas [F] 28 A1
Blajan [F] 36 F3
Blâmont [F] 22 D2
Blangy–sur–Bresle [F] 12 B1
Blankenberge [B] 4 D3
Blanquefort [F] 30 C1
Blanzac [F] 24 C4

Blaye [F] 30 C1
Bléneau [F] 20 A3
Blérancourt [F] 12 D3
Bléré [F] 18 C3
Blériot–Plage [F] 4 B3
Blesle [F] 32 E2
Bletterans [F] 28 B3
Bliesbruck–Reinheim, Parc
   Archéol. de– [F] 22 D1
Bligny–sur–Ouche [F] 26 F2
Blois [F] 18 D3
Blokzijl [NL] 2 D3
Bocholt [B] 6 C4
Bocognano [F] 44 B3
Bodegraven [NL] 2 B4
Boëge [F] 28 C4
Boën [F] 34 A1
Bohal [F] 16 C1
Bohain–en–Vermandois [F]
   12 E2
Bois–du–Four [F] 32 D4
Bolbec [F] 10 E2
Bollène [F] 40 D1
Bologne [F] 20 E3
Bolsward [NL] 2 C2

Bonaguil, Château de– [F]
   30 F3
Bonhomme, Col du– [F] 22 D3
Bonifacio [F] 44 B4
Bonlieu [F] 28 C3
Bonnat [F] 26 B3
Bonnesvalyn [F] 12 D4
Bonnétable [F] 18 C1
Bonneval [F] 18 D2
Bonneval–sur–Arc [F] 34 F2
Bonneville [F] 28 C4
Bonnières [F] 12 A3
Bonnieux [F] 40 E2
Bonny–sur–Loire [F] 18 F3
Bonport, Abbaye de– [F] 12 A3
Boom [B] 4 F4
Boos [F] 12 A2
Borculo [NL] 6 D2
Bordeaux [F] 30 C2
Bordères [F] 36 E3
Borger [NL] 2 E3
Bormes–les–Mimosas [F]
   42 B4
Bort–les–Orgues [F] 32 D1
Bosc–Mesnil [F] 12 A2

Bosgouet [F] 10 F2
Boskoop [NL] 2 B4
Bouaye [F] 16 D3
Bouchair [F] 12 C2
Bouconville–sur–Madt [F]
   20 F1
Bouesse [F] 26 A2
Bouges–le–Château [F] 18 D4
Bouguenais [F] 16 D3
Bouillon [B] 14 A3
Bouilly [F] 20 C2
Boulay–Moselle [F] 14 C4
Bouligny [F] 14 B4
Boulogne–sur–Gesse [F] 36 F3
Boulogne–sur–Mer [F] 4 B4
Bouloire [F] 18 C2
Boumois, Château de– [F]
   18 A3
Bouniagues [F] 30 E2
Bourbon–Lancy [F] 26 E2
Bourbon–l'Archambault [F]
   26 C2
Bourbonne–les–Bains [F]
   20 F3
Bourbourg [F] 4 C3

Bourbriac [F] 8 D3
Bourdeaux [F] 34 C4
Bourdeilles [F] 30 E1
Bourg [F] 30 D1
Bourg–Achard [F] 10 F2
Bourganeuf [F] 26 A3
Bourg–Argental [F] 34 B2
Bourg–de–Péage [F] 34 C3
Bourg–en–Bresse [F] 28 B4
Bourges [F] 26 C1
Bourg–et–Comin [F] 12 E3
Bourg–Lastic [F] 26 B4
Bourg–Madame [F] 38 C4
Bourgneuf–en–Retz [F] 16 D3
Bourgogne [F] 12 E3
Bourgoin–Jallieu [F] 34 C2
Bourg–St–Andéol [F] 34 B4
Bourg–St–Maurice [F] 34 E2
Bourgtheroulde–Infreville [F]
   10 F3
Bourgueil [F] 18 B3
Bourideys [F] 30 C3
Bourmont [F] 20 E3
Bourneville [F] 10 F2
Bournezeau [F] 16 D4

Boussac [F] 26 B3
Boussens [F] 38 B2
Bouvignes [B] 14 A2
Bouvron [F] 16 D2
Bouxwiller [F] 22 E2
Bouzonville [F] 14 C4
Boxmeer [NL] 6 C3
Boxtel [NL] 6 B3
Bozel [F] 34 E2
Bozouls [F] 32 D3
Bozouls, Trou de– [F] 32 D3
Bra [B] 14 C2
Bracieux [F] 18 D3
Braine [F] 12 D3
Brakel [B] 4 E4
Bram [F] 38 D2
Brancion [F] 26 F3
Brandon [F] 26 F3
Branne [F] 30 D2
Brantôme [F] 24 D4
Bras–d'Asse [F] 40 F2
Brassac [F] 38 E2
Brassac–Jumeaux [F] 32 E1
Brasschaat [B] 4 F3
Bras–sur–Meuse [F] 14 B4
Braus, Col de– [F] 42 D2
Bravone [F] 44 C2
Bray–sur–Seine [F] 20 B2
Bray–sur–Somme [F] 12 D2
Brécey [F] 10 C3
Brécy [F] 18 E4
Brecht [B] 6 A3
Breda [NL] 6 B3
Bréhal [F] 10 B3
Breil–sur–Roya [F] 42 D2
Brénod [F] 28 B4
Bresdon [F] 24 C3
Breskens [NL] 4 E3
Bresles [F] 12 C3
Bressuire [F] 16 F4
Brest [F] 8 B3
Breteau [F] 18 F3
Bretenoux [F] 32 B2
Bretesche, Château de la– [F] 16 C2
Breteuil [F] 10 F4
Breteuil [F] 12 C2
Brétignolles–Sur–Mer [F] 16 C4
Breukelen Ut [NL] 2 B4
Brézolles [F] 10 F4
Briançon [F] 34 E3
Briare [F] 18 F3
Bricquebec [F] 10 B1
Brie–Comte–Robert [F] 18 F1
Brielle [NL] 4 F2
Brienne–le–Château [F] 20 D2
Briey [F] 14 C4
Brignogan–Plage [F] 8 B2
Brignoles [F] 40 F3
Brignoud [F] 34 D2
Brinay [F] 18 E4
Brinon [F] 20 B4
Brionne [F] 10 F3
Brioude [F] 32 E2
Brioux–sur–Boutonne [F] 24 C2
Briouze [F] 10 D3
Brissac–Quincé [F] 16 F3
Brive–la–Gaillarde [F] 32 B2
Broglie [F] 10 E3
Brommat [F] 32 D3
Bron [F] 34 C1
Broons [F] 8 E4
Brossac [F] 24 C4
Brou [F] 18 D2
Brouage [F] 24 B3
Brouis, Col de– [F] 42 D2
Brouvelieures [F] 22 C3
Brouwershaven [NL] 4 E2
Bruère–Allichamps [F] 26 C2
Brugge [B] 4 D3
Brûlon [F] 18 A2

Brumath [F] 22 E2
Brummen [NL] 6 D2
Brunehamel [F] 12 F2
Bruniquel [F] 32 B4
Brunssum [NL] 6 C4
Brussel / Bruxelles [B] 4 F4
Bruxelles / Brussel [B] 4 F4
Bruyères [F] 22 C3
Bubry [F] 8 C4
Buchy [F] 12 A2
Bucquoy [F] 12 D1
Bugeat [F] 26 A4
Buis–les–Baronnies [F] 40 E1
Buitenpost [NL] 2 D2
Bulat–Pestivien [F] 8 C3
Bunleix [F] 26 B4
Buoux, Fort de– [F] 40 E2
Burgh–Haamstede [NL] 4 E2
Burie [F] 24 C3
Buron, Château de– [F] 32 E1
Bussang [F] 22 C4
Bussang, Col de– [F] 22 D4
Bussum [NL] 2 B4
Bütgenbach [B] 14 C2
Buxy [F] 26 F3
Buzançais [F] 26 A1
Buzancy [F] 14 A3

C

Cabourg [F] 10 D2
Cabrerets [F] 32 B3
Cadenet [F] 40 E2
Cadeuil [F] 24 B3
Cadillac [F] 30 D2
Caen [F] 10 D2
Cagnes–sur–Mer [F] 42 C3
Cahors [F] 32 B3
Cajarc [F] 32 B3
Calacuccia [F] 44 B2
Calais [F] 4 B3
Calenzana [F] 44 B2
Calignac [F] 30 E3
Callac [F] 8 C3
Calvi [F] 44 B2
Camarès [F] 38 E1
Camaret–sur–Mer [F] 8 A3
Cambo–les–Bains [F] 36 C2
Cambrai [F] 12 D1
Cambremer [F] 10 E3
Campan [F] 36 E3
Canaples [F] 12 C1
Cancale [F] 8 F3
Cancon [F] 30 E3
Candé [F] 16 E2
Canet [F] 40 B2
Canet–Plage [F] 38 E4
Cannes [F] 42 C3
Cany–Barville [F] 10 F2
Capbreton [F] 30 A4
Cap–d'Ail [F] 42 D3
Capdenac–Gare [F] 32 C3
Capendu [F] 38 D3
Capens [F] 38 B2
Capestang [F] 38 E2
Cap Ferret [F] 30 B2
Capo Cavallo [F] 44 A2
Captieux [F] 30 D3
Caraman [F] 38 C2
Carantec [F] 8 C2
Carbon–Blanc [F] 30 C1
Carbonne [F] 38 B2
Carcans [F] 30 C1
Carcans–Plage [F] 24 A4
Carcassonne [F] 38 D2
Carcès [F] 40 F3
Carennac [F] 32 B2

Carentan [F] 10 C2
Cargèse [F] 44 A2
Carhaix–Plouguer [F] 8 C3
Carignan [F] 14 B3
Carling [F] 22 D1
Carmaux [F] 32 C4
Carnac [F] 16 B1
Caro [F] 16 C1
Carpentras [F] 40 D1
Carquefou [F] 16 D3
Carqueiranne [F] 40 F4
Carro [F] 40 D3
Carros [F] 42 C2
Carrouges [F] 10 D4
Carry–le–Rouet [F] 40 D3
Carteret [F] 10 B2
Casamozza [F] 44 C2
Cassagnes–Bégonhès [F] 32 C4
Cassel [F] 4 C4
Cassis [F] 40 E3
Cassuéjouls [F] 32 D3
Castanet–Tolosan [F] 38 C2
Casteau [B] 12 F1
Castelbouc [F] 32 E4
Casteljaloux [F] 30 D3
Castellane [F] 42 B2
Castelmoron [F] 30 E3
Castelnau [F] 32 B2
Castelnaudary [F] 38 D2
Castelnau–de–Médoc [F] 30 C1
Castelnau–de–Montmiral [F] 32 B4
Castelnau d'Estretefonds [F] 38 C1
Castelnau–Magnoac [F] 36 F3
Castelnau–Montratier [F] 30 F3
Castelsarrasin [F] 30 F4
Castets [F] 30 B3
Castillon–la–Bataille [F] 30 D2
Castillonnès [F] 30 E2
Castres [F] 38 D1
Castricum [NL] 2 B3
Castries [F] 40 C2
Cateraggio [F] 44 C3
Catus [F] 32 A3
Caudebec–en–Caux [F] 10 F2
Caudeval [F] 38 C3
Caudry [F] 12 E2
Caumont [F] 10 C2
Caumont [F] 38 B2
Caunes–Minervois [F] 38 D2
Cauro [F] 44 B3
Caussade [F] 32 B4
Causse de la– [F]
Cauterets [F] 36 D3
Cauville [F] 10 E2
Cavaillon [F] 40 D2
Cavalaire–sur–Mer [F] 42 B4
Cavalière [F] 42 B4
Caylus [F] 32 B3
Cayrols [F] 32 C2
Cazals [F] 30 F3
Cazaubon [F] 30 D4
Cazeneuve, Château de– [F] 30 D3
Cazères [F] 38 B2
Ceillac [F] 34 E4
Celles [B] 4 D4
Celles–sur–Belle [F] 24 D2
Celsoy [F] 20 E3
Centuri [F] 44 C1
Céret [F] 38 D4
Cerfontaine [B] 12 F2
Cérilly [F] 26 C2
Cerisiers [F] 20 B2
Cerizay [F] 16 E4
Cernay [F] 22 D4
Cerniébaud [F] 28 C3
Cervione [F] 44 C2
Cessenon–sur–Orb [F] 38 E2
Ceyrat [F] 32 E1

Ceyzériat [F] 28 B4
Chaalis, Abbaye de– [F] 12 C3
Chabanais [F] 24 E3
Chabeuil [F] 34 B3
Chablis [F] 20 C3
Chabreloche [F] 26 D4
Chabris [F] 18 D4
Chagny [F] 28 A2
Chailland [F] 18 F1
Chaillé–les–Marais [F] 24 B2
Chailley–Turny [F] 20 B3
Chailluz, Fort de– [F] 28 C2
Chalabre [F] 38 C3
Chalais [F] 24 C4
Challes–les–Eaux [F] 34 D2
Chalonnes–sur–Loire [F] 16 E3
Châlons–en–Champagne [F] 20 D1
Chalon–sur–Saône [F] 28 A2
Châlus [F] 24 E4
Chalusset, Château de– [F] 24 F4
Chambéret [F] 24 F4
Chambéry [F] 34 D2
Chambilly [F] 26 E3
Chambley–Bussières [F] 20 F1
Chambon–sur–Lac [F] 32 D1
Chambon–sur–Voueize [F] 26 B3
Chambord [F] 18 D3
Chambord, Parc de– [F] 18 D3
Chamonix–Mont–Blanc [F] 34 F1
Champagnac–le–Vieux [F] 32 E2
Champagne–Mouton [F] 24 D3
Champagnole [F] 28 C3
Champaubert [F] 20 C1
Champdeniers [F] 24 C2
Champ du Feu [F] 22 D3
Champ de la Bataille, Château du– [F] 10 F3
Champeix [F] 32 E1
Champier [F] 34 C2
Champigné [F] 16 F2
Champigny–sur–Veude [F] 18 B4
Champillon [F] 12 E4
Champlitte [F] 20 E4
Champlon [B] 14 B2
Champrond–en–Gâtine [F] 18 D1
Champtoceaux [F] 16 E3
Chamrousse [F] 34 D3
Chanaleilles [F] 32 E3
Chanas [F] 34 B2
Chantelle [F] 26 D3
Chantemerle [F] 34 E3
Chantilly [F] 12 C3
Chantonnay [F] 16 E4
Chaource [F] 20 C3
Chapelle–Royale [F] 18 D2
Charavines [F] 34 C2
Charbonnières–les–Bains [F] 34 B1
Charenton–du–Cher [F] 26 C2
Charité, Abbaye de la– [F] 28 C1
Charleville–Mézières [F] 14 A3
Charlieu [F] 26 E4
Charly [F] 26 C2
Charly [F] 12 D4
Charmes [F] 22 C3
Charny [F] 20 A3
Charolles [F] 26 E3
Chârost [F] 26 B1
Charpentry [F] 14 A4
Charroux [F] 24 D3
Chartres [F] 18 D1

Chassant [F] 18 D1
Chasseneuil–s.–Bonnieure [F] 24 D3
Chasse sur Rhone [F] 34 B2
Chassigny [F] 20 E4
Château–Arnoux [F] 40 F2
Châteaubourg [F] 16 E1
Châteaubriant [F] 16 E2
Château–Chinon [F] 26 E2
Château–du–Loir [F] 18 B2
Châteaudun [F] 18 D2
Châteaugiron [F] 16 E1
Château–Gontier [F] 16 F2
Château–Landon [F] 18 F2
Château–la–Vallière [F] 18 B3
Château–l'Évêque [F] 30 E1
Châteaulin [F] 8 B3
Châteaumeillant [F] 26 B2
Châteauneuf [F] 24 C3
Châteauneuf–de–Randon [F] 32 E3
Châteauneuf–du–Faou [F] 8 C3
Châteauneuf–du–Pape [F] 40 D1
Châteauneuf–en–Thymerais [F] 10 F4
Châteauneuf–sur–Cher [F] 26 B2
Châteauneuf–sur–Sarthe [F] 16 F2
Châteauponsac [F] 24 F3
Château–Porcien [F] 12 F3
Château–Queyras [F] 34 E4
Château–Regnault [F] 14 A2
Châteaurenard [F] 20 A3
Château–Renault [F] 18 C3
Châteauroux [F] 26 A2
Château–Salins [F] 22 C2
Château–Thierry [F] 12 D4
Châteauvillain [F] 20 D3
Châtel [F] 28 D4
Châtelaillon–Plage [F] 24 B2
Châtelet [B] 14 A1
Châtelguyon [F] 26 C4
Châtellerault [F] 24 E1
Châtelus–Malvaleix [F] 26 B3
Châtenois [F] 20 F3
Châtillon–Coligny [F] 18 F3
Châtillon–en–Bazois [F] 26 E2
Châtillon–en–Diois [F] 34 C4
Châtillon–sur–Chalaronne [F] 28 A4
Châtillon–sur–Indre [F] 18 C4
Châtillon–sur–Loire [F] 18 F3
Châtillon–sur–Marne [F] 12 E4
Châtillon–sur–Seine [F] 20 D3
Châtre, Église de– [F] 24 C3
Chaudes–Aigues [F] 32 D3
Chauffailles [F] 26 E3
Chaufour–lès–Bonnières [F] 12 A3
Chaumergy [F] 28 B2
Chaumont [F] 20 E3
Chaumont–sur–Aire [F] 20 E1
Chaumont–sur–Loire [F] 18 C3
Chaunay [F] 24 D2
Chauny [F] 12 D3
Chaussin [F] 28 B2
Chauvigny [F] 24 E2
Chaux–Neuve [F] 28 C3
Chazelles–sur–Lyon [F] 34 B1
Chef–Boutonne [F] 24 D2
Chémery–sur–Bar [F] 14 A3
Chemillé [F] 16 E3
Chemin [F] 28 B2
Chêne–Pignier [F] 24 E3
Chénérailles [F] 26 B3
Chenonceaux [F] 18 C3
Cherbourg [F] 10 B1
Chéroy [F] 20 A2
Cherveix–Cubas [F] 32 A1

Cherves–Richemont [F] 24 C3
Chevagnes [F] 26 D2
Chevanceaux [F] 24 C4
Chevilly, Château de– [F] 18 E2
Chevreuse [F] 12 B4
Chézal–Benoît [F] 26 B2
Chigny [F] 12 E2
Chimay [B] 12 F2
Chinon [F] 18 B3
Chisa [F] 44 B3
Cholet [F] 16 E3
Chorges [F] 34 D4
Chouvigny, Gorges de– [F] 26 C3
Choye [F] 28 C1
Chvagnes–en–Paillers [F] 16 D4
Cibourre [F] 36 B2
Cierp–Gaud [F] 36 F3
Ciney [B] 14 B2
Cintegabelle [F] 38 C2
Cirey [F] 22 D2
Ciron [F] 24 F2
Cîteaux, Abbaye de– [F] 28 B2
Civray [F] 24 D2
Civrieux–d'Azergues [F] 34 B1
Clairvaux–les–Lacs [F] 28 C3
Clamecy [F] 20 B4
Clamerey [F] 28 A1
Clamouse, Grotte de– [F] 40 B2
Clécy [F] 10 D3
Clefmont [F] 20 E3
Clefs [F] 18 B2
Clelles [F] 34 C3
Cléon–d'Andran [F] 34 B4
Clères [F] 12 A2
Clermont [F] 12 C3
Clermont–de–Beauregarde [F] 30 E2
Clermont–en–Argonne [F] 14 A4
Clermont–Ferrand [F] 26 C4
Clermont–l'Hérault [F] 38 F2
Clerval [F] 28 D2
Clervaux [L] 14 C2
Cléry [F] 18 D3
Clesse [F] 16 F4
Clisson [F] 16 E3
Clohars–Carnöet [F] 8 C4
Cloyes–sur–le–Loir [F] 18 D2
Cluny [F] 26 F3
Cluses [F] 34 E1
Coflans [F] 34 E2
Cognac [F] 24 C3
Cogolin [F] 42 B4
Cohiniac [F] 8 D3
Colembert [F] 4 B4
Coligny [F] 28 B3
Collinée [F] 8 D4
Collioure [F] 38 E4
Collonges [F] 28 C4
Collonges–la–Rouge [F] 32 B2
Colmar [F] 22 D3
Colmars [F] 42 B2
Cologne [F] 38 B1
Colombey–les–Belles [F] 20 F2
Colombey–les–Deux–Églises [F] 20 D3
Colomiers [F] 38 C1
Combeaufontaine [F] 20 F4
Combourg [F] 8 F4
Combronde [F] 26 C4
Commentry [F] 26 C3
Commequiers [F] 16 D4
Commercy [F] 20 F2
Compiègne [F] 12 C3
Comps–sur–Artuby [F] 42 B3
Conca [F] 44 B3
Concarneau [F] 8 B4

Conches–en–Ouche [F] 10 F3
Condat [F] 32 D2
Condé–en–Brie [F] 12 D4
Condé–sur–Noireau [F] 10 D3
Condom [F] 30 D4
Condrieu [F] 34 B2
Conflans en Jarnisy [F] 14 B4
Conflans–sur–Lanterne [F] 22 B4
Confolens [F] 24 E3
Conlie [F] 18 B1
Connantre [F] 20 C1
Connerré [F] 18 C2
Conques [F] 32 C3
Constantine [F] 14 B4
Contay [F] 12 C2
Contins–Plage [F] 30 B3
Contres [F] 18 D3
Contrexéville [F] 20 F3
Conty [F] 12 C2
Coray [F] 8 B4
Corbeil–Essonnes [F] 18 F1
Corbeny [F] 12 E3
Corbie [F] 12 C2
Corbigny [F] 26 E1
Corcieux [F] 22 D3
Corconne [F] 40 B2
Cordes [F] 32 B4
Corlay [F] 8 D3
Cormainville [F] 18 D2
Cormeilles [F] 10 E3
Cormery [F] 18 C3
Cornimont [F] 22 C3
Corps [F] 34 D3
Corre [F] 20 F3
Corseul [F] 8 E3
Corte [F] 44 B2
Cosne–Cours–sur–Loire [F] 18 F4
Cosne d'Allier [F] 26 C3
Cossé–le–Vivien [F] 16 F2
Cotignac [F] 40 F3
Couches [F] 26 F2
Coucy–le–Château–Auffrique [F] 12 D3
Coudray–Montbault, Château de– [F] 16 F3
Couflenz [F] 38 B3
Cougnac, Grottes de– [F] 32 B2
Couhé [F] 24 D2
Couilly [F] 12 C4
Couiza [F] 38 D3
Coulanges–la–Vineuse [F] 20 B3
Coulmier–le–Sec [F] 20 D3
Coulommiers [F] 20 B1
Coulon [F] 24 C2
Coulonges [F] 24 C1
Couptrain [F] 10 D4
Courboyer, Manoir de– [F] 18 C1
Courceau [F] 20 D4
Courchevel [F] 34 E2
Cour–Cheverny [F] 18 D3
Courçon [F] 24 C2
Cour–et–Buis [F] 34 C2
Courgains [F] 18 B1
Courpière [F] 32 E1
Courrière [B] 14 A1
Coursan [F] 38 E3
Courseulles–sur–Mer [F] 10 D2
Cours–la–Ville [F] 26 E4
Courson–les–Carrières [F] 20 B3
Courtacon [F] 20 B1
Courtanvaux, Château de– [F] 18 C2
Courteilles [F] 10 E3
Courtenay [F] 20 A2
Courtelevant [F] 28 E1

Courtomer [F] 10 E4
Courtrail (Kortrijk) [B] 4 D4
Courville [F] 18 D1
Coutances [F] 10 B2
Couterne [F] 10 D4
Coutevroult [F] 12 C4
Coutras [F] 30 D1
Couvin [B] 12 F2
Cox [F] 38 B1
Cozes [F] 24 B3
Cozzano [F] 44 B3
Craon [F] 16 E2
Craponne–sur–Arzon [F] 32 F2
Crêches–sur–Saône [F] 26 F4
Crécy [F] 12 C4
Crécy–en–Ponthieu [F] 12 B1
Crécy–sur–Serre [F] 12 E3
Creil [F] 12 C3
Crémieu [F] 34 C1
Créon [F] 30 D2
Crépy–en–Valois [F] 12 C3
Crésantignes [F] 20 C2–3
Crespin [F] 12 E1
Cressensac [F] 32 B2
Crest [F] 34 B3
Creutzwald [F] 14 D4
Crevecœur–en–Auge [F] 10 E3
Crevecœur [F] 12 B2
Crillon [F] 12 B2
Crocq [F] 26 B4
Croix Haute, Col de la– [F] 34 C4
Cro–Magnon [F] 30 F2
Crozant [F] 26 A2
Crozon [F] 8 B3
Cruas [F] 34 B3
Cruseilles [F] 34 E1
Cruzy [F] 38 E2
Cruzy [F] 20 D3
Cuers [F] 40 F3
Cugnon–sur–Semois [B] 14 B3
Cuhom [F] 4 C4
Cuijk [NL] 6 C2
Cuillé [F] 16 E1
Cuiseaux [F] 28 B3
Cuisery [F] 28 A3
Culan [F] 26 B2
Culemborg [NL] 6 B2
Culoz [F] 34 D1
Cunault [F] 18 A3
Curel [F] 40 E1
Cusset [F] 26 D3
Custines [F] 22 C2
Cutting [F] 22 D2
Cuvilly [F] 12 C3

D

Dabo [F] 22 D2
Dabo, Roch. de– [F] 22 D2
Dalstein [F] 14 C4
Daluis, Gorges de– [F] 42 C2
Dammartin–en–Goële [F] 12 C4
Damparis [F] 28 B2
Dampierre [F] 12 B4
Dampierre [F] 28 C2
Dampierre–sur–Boutonne [F] 24 C2
Dampierre–sur–Salon [F] 20 E4
Damville [F] 10 F4
Damvillers [F] 14 B4
Dangé–St–Romain [F] 18 B4
Dannemarie [F] 28 E1
Daon [F] 16 F2

Daoulas [F] 8 B3
Dargilan, Grotte de– [F] 32 E4
Darney [F] 20 F3
Dax [F] 30 B4
Deauville [F] 10 E2
Decazeville [F] 32 C3
Decines [F] 34 C1
Decize [F] 26 D2
De Cocksdorp [NL] 2 B2
Dedemsvaart [NL] 2 D3
Defile de l'Ecluse [F] 28 C4
De Haan [B] 4 D3
Deinze [B] 4 E4
De Koog [NL] 2 B2
De Kooy [NL] 2 B2
Delden [NL] 2 E4
Delft [NL] 2 A4
Delfzijl [NL] 2 E2
Delle [F] 28 E1
Delme [F] 22 C1
Delouze–Rosières [F] 20 E2
Demigny [F] 28 A2
Demoiselles, Grotte des– [F] 40 B1
Denain [F] 12 E1
Den Burg [NL] 2 B2
Dendermonde [B] 4 E4
Denekamp [NL] 2 E4
Den Haag [NL] 2 A4
Den Helder [NL] 2 B2
Den Oever [NL] 2 C2
De Panne [B] 4 C3
Derval [F] 16 D2
Descartes [F] 18 B4
Desvres [F] 4 B4
Deurne [NL] 6 C3
Deventer [NL] 2 D4
Die [F] 34 C3
Diekirch [L] 14 C3
Dienne [F] 32 D2
Dieppe [F] 12 A1
Dieren [NL] 6 D2
Diest [B] 6 B4
Dieue–sur–Meuse [F] 20 E1
Dieulefit [F] 34 B4
Dieulouard [F] 22 C2
Dieuze [F] 22 D2
Diever [NL] 2 D3
Differdange [L] 14 C3
Dignac [F] 24 D4
Digne–les–Bains [F] 42 B2
Digny [F] 18 D1
Digoin [F] 26 E3
Dijon [F] 28 B1
Diksmuide [B] 4 D3
Dinan [F] 8 E3
Dinant [B] 14 A2
Dinard [F] 8 E3
Dinozé [F] 22 C3
Disneyland [F] 12 C4
Dives–sur–Mer [F] 10 D2
Divonne–les–Bains [F] 28 C4
Dizy–le–Gros [F] 12 E3
Dochamps [F] 14 B2
Doesburg [NL] 6 D2
Doetinchem [NL] 6 D2
Dokkum [NL] 2 D2
Dol–de–Bretagne [F] 8 F3
Dole [F] 28 B2
Dombasle [F] 22 C2
Dombret–le–Sec [F] 20 F3
Domburg [NL] 4 E2
Domèvre–en–Haye [F] 20 F2
Domfront [F] 10 C4
Domme [F] 30 F2
Dompaire [F] 22 C3
Dompierre [F] 26 D3
Dompierre–du–Chemin [F] 10 B4
Dompierre–sur–Besbre [F] 26 D3
Domrémy–la–Pucelle [F] 20 F2

Dontilly [F] 20 B2
Donzenac [F] 32 B1
Donzère [F] 34 B4
Donzy [F] 20 A4
Doorn [NL] 6 C2
Dordives [F] 18 F2
Dordrecht [NL] 6 B2
Dormans [F] 12 E4
Dornas [F] 34 A3
Dornes [F] 26 D2
Dortan [F] 28 B4
Douai [F] 12 D1
Douamont, Fort du– [F] 14 B4
Douarnenez [F] 8 B3
Douchy [F] 20 A3
Doucier [F] 28 C3
Doudeville [F] 10 F2
Doué–la–Fontaine [F] 16 F3
Doulaincourt [F] 20 E2
Doulevant–le–Château [F] 20 D2
Doullens [F] 12 C1
Dourdan [F] 18 E1
Dourgne [F] 38 D2
Doussard [F] 34 E1–2
Douvaine [F] 28 C4
Douzy [F] 14 A3
Dozulé [F] 10 E2
Drachten [NL] 2 D2
Dragon, Caverne du– [F] 12 E3
Draguignan [F] 42 B3
Dreux [F] 12 A4
Driebergen [NL] 6 C2
Drionville [F] 4 B4
Dronten [NL] 2 C3
Drusenheim [F] 22 E2
Druten [NL] 6 C2
Ducey [F] 10 B3
Duclair [F] 10 F2
Dudelange [L] 14 C4
Duingt [F] 34 E1
Dun [F] 14 A4
Dunkerque [F] 4 C3
Dunkerque Ouest [F] 4 C3
Dun–le–Palestel [F] 26 A3
Dun–sur–Auron [F] 26 C2
Durance [F] 30 D3
Duras [F] 30 D2
Durban–Corbières [F] 38 E3
Durbuy [B] 14 B2
Durtal [F] 18 A2
Dwingeloo [NL] 2 D3

E

Eaux–Bonnes [F] 36 D3
Eaux–Chaudes [F] 36 D3
Eauze [F] 30 D4
Ebreuil [F] 26 C3
Echallon [F] 28 B4
Échourgnac [F] 30 E1
Echternach [L] 14 C3
Ecole Valentine [F] 28 C2
Ecommoy [F] 18 B2
Ecouis [F] 12 A3
Ecoust–St–Mein [F] 12 D1
Ecueillé [F] 18 C4
Ecury [F] 20 D1
Edam [NL] 2 B3
Ede [NL] 6 C2
Édon [F] 24 D4
Eeklo [B] 4 E3
Eelde [NL] 2 E2
Een [NL] 2 D2
Eghezée [B] 14 B1
Egletons [F] 32 C1
Egmond aan Zee [NL] 2 B3

Eguzon [F] 26 A2
Ehnen [L] 14 C3
Eibergen [NL] 6 D2
Eindhoven [NL] 6 C3
Elbeuf [F] 10 F3
Elburg [NL] 2 C4
Elne [F] 38 E4
Elst [NL] 6 C2
Elven, Tour d'– [F] 16 C1
Emberménil [F] 22 C2
Embrun [F] 34 E4
Emmeloord [NL] 2 C3
Emmen [NL] 2 E3
Englefontaine [F] 12 E1
Enkhuizen [NL] 2 C3
Ennezat [F] 26 D4
Enschede [NL] 2 E4
Ensisheim [F] 22 D4
Entraigues [F] 18 D4
Entrains–sur–Nohain [F] 20 B4
Entraygues–sur–Truyère [F]
    32 C3
Entrevaux [F] 42 C2
Eoux [F] 38 B2
Epannes [F] 24 C2
Epe [NL] 2 D4
Épernay [F] 12 E4
Épernon [F] 18 E1
Épinal [F] 22 C3
Epiry [F] 26 E1
Epône [F] 12 B4
Épuisay [F] 18 C2
Erbalunga [F] 44 C1
Ermelo [NL] 2 D4
Ermenonville [F] 12 C3
Ermitage, Grotte de l'– [F]
    28 B2
Ernée [F] 10 C4
Erquy [F] 8 E3
Erstein [F] 22 E3
Ervy–le–Châtel [F] 20 C3
Esch–sur–Alzette [L] 14 C3
Esch–sur–Sûre [L] 14 C3
Escos [F] 36 C2
Esnandes [F] 24 B2
Esnouvenaux [F] 20 E3
Espalion [F] 32 D3
Espelette [F] 36 B2
Espezel [F] 38 C3
Esplantas [F] 32 E3
Esprels [F] 28 D1
Essertaux [F] 12 C2
Essoyes [F] 20 D3
Essuilles [F] 12 C3
Estagel [F] 38 E3
Estaing [F] 32 D3
Estaires [F] 4 C4
Estang [F] 30 D4
Esternay [F] 20 C1
Estissac [F] 20 C2
Estrées–St–Denis [F] 12 C3
Étables–sur–Mer [F] 8 D3
Etagnac [F] 24 E3
Etain [F] 14 B4
Etalle [B] 14 B3
Étampes [F] 18 E1
Étang–sur–Arroux [F] 26 E2
Etaples [F] 4 B4
Etoges [F] 20 C1
Eton [F] 14 B4
Etréaupont [F] 12 E2
Etrepagny [F] 12 B3
Etretat [F] 10 E2
Ettelbruck [L] 14 C3
Eu [F] 12 B1
Eugénie–les–Bains [F] 30 C4
Eupen [B] 14 C1
Europoort [NL] 2 A4
Evaux–les–Bains [F] 26 B3
Evian [F] 28 D4
Evisa [F] 44 B2
Evran [F] 8 E4

Evreux [F] 10 F3
Evron [F] 18 A1
Evry [F] 18 F1
Excideuil [F] 30 F1
Exmes [F] 10 E4
Eyguières [F] 40 D2
Eygurande [F] 26 B4
Eylie [F] 36 F4
Eymet [F] 30 E2
Eymoutiers [F] 26 A4

Facture [F] 30 C2
Fageole, Col de la– [F] 32 E2
Fains le Sources [F] 20 E1
Falaise [F] 10 D3
Falkenstein, Château de– [F]
    22 E1
Fanjeaux [F] 38 D2
Farcheville, Château de– [F]
    18 F1
Farébersviller [F] 22 D1
Faucille, Col de la– [F]
    28 C4
Faucogney–et–la–Mer [F]
    22 C4
Faulquemont [F] 22 C1
Fauville [F] 10 F2
Faverges [F] 34 E2
Faverney [F] 20 F4
Favone [F] 44 C3
Fayence [F] 42 B3
Fayet [F] 38 E1
Fayl–Billot [F] 20 E4
Fay–sur–Lignon [F] 34 A3
Fécamp [F] 10 E2
Felletin [F] 26 B4
Fénétrange [F] 22 D2
Feneu [F] 16 F2
Fer a Cheval, Cirque du– [F]
    28 C2
Fère, Château de– [F] 12 D4
Fère–Champenoise [F] 20 C1
Fère–en–Tardenois [F]
    12 D4
Ferrette [F] 28 E1
Ferrières [F] 18 F2
Ferrières–sur–Sichon [F]
    26 D4
Feu, Roche du– [F] 8 B3
Feurs [F] 34 B1
Fier, Gorges du– [F] 34 D1
Figari [F] 44 B4
Figeac [F] 32 C3
Filitosa [F] 44 B3
Firminy [F] 34 A2
Fismes [F] 12 E3
Flagy [F] 22 B4
Flaine [F] 34 F1
Flaran [F] 30 D4
Flaugeac [F] 30 E2
Flavigny–sur–Moselle [F]
    22 C2
Fléchin [F] 4 C4
Fleckenstein, Château de– [F]
    22 E1
Flers [F] 10 D3
Fleurance [F] 30 E4
Fleuré [F] 24 E2
Fleurus [B] 14 A1
Fleury [F] 12 B4
Flins [F] 12 B4
Flize [F] 14 A3
Flogny–la–Chapelle [F] 20 C3
Florac [F] 32 E4
Florange [F] 14 C4

Florennes [B] 14 A2
Florenville [B] 14 B3
Flumet [F] 34 E1
Foix [F] 38 C3
Folelli [F] 44 C2
Fondamente [F] 38 F1
Fontainebleau [F] 18 F2
Fontaine–de–Vaucluse [F]
    40 D2
Fontaine–Française [F]
    20 E4
Fontaine Guérard, Abbaye de–
    [F] 12 A3
Fontaine Henry, Château de–
    [F] 10 D2
Fontaine–le–Dun [F] 10 F2
Fontaine–sur–Coole [F]
    20 D1
Fontenay, Abbaye de– [F]
    20 C4
Fontenay–le–Comte [F]
    24 C1
Fontenay–Trésigny [F] 20 B1
Fontevraud–l'Abbaye [F]
    18 B3
Fontfroide, Abbaye de– [F]
    38 E3
Fontgombault [F] 24 F2
Font–Romeu [F] 38 C4
Fontvieille [F] 40 D2
Forbach [F] 22 D1
Forcalquier [F] 40 F2
Forges–les–Eaux [F] 12 B2
Formerie [F] 12 B2
Formiguères [F] 38 C4
Fos [F] 36 F4
Fosses [F] 14 A1
Fos–sur–Mer [F] 40 D3
Foucarmont [F] 12 B2
Fouesnant [F] 8 B4
Fougères [F] 10 B4
Fougerolles [F] 22 C4
Foulain [F] 20 E3
Fouras [F] 24 B2
Fourcès [F] 30 D4
Fourmies [F] 12 E2
Fourneaux [F] 26 B3
Fournels [F] 32 D3
Fourquet [F] 30 E3
Fours [F] 26 E2
Fraize [F] 22 D3
Framzelle [F] 4 B4
Francardo [F] 44 B2
Franeker [NL] 2 C2
Frangy [F] 34 D1
Frasne [F] 28 C3
Frayssinet [F] 32 B3
Fréjus [F] 42 B3
Fresnay–sur–Sarthe [F]
    18 B1
Fresnes [F] 12 D1
Fresnes [F] 20 F3
Fresnes–en–Woëvre [F]
    20 F1
Fréteval [F] 18 D2
Fretigney–et–Velloreille [F]
    28 C1
Frévent [F] 12 C1
Froissy [F] 12 C2
Fromental [F] 10 D3
Fromentine F16 C3
Fromy [F] 14 B3
Fronsac [F] 36 F3
Frontignan [F] 40 B2
Fronton [F] 32 A4
Frossay [F] 16 D3
Fumay [F] 14 A2
Fumel [F] 30 F3
Furnes (Veurne) [B] 4 C3

G

Gaasbeek [B] 4 F4
Gabarret [F] 30 D3
Gacé [F] 10 E3
Gaël [F] 8 E4
Gaillac [F] 38 D1
Gaillon [F] 12 A3
Galan [F] 36 E3
Galéria [F] 44 A2
Gallargues [F] 40 C2
Gard, Pont du– [F] 40 C2
Gardanne [F] 40 E3
Garein [F] 30 C3
Gargas, Grotte de– [F] 36 F3
Gargilesse–Dampierre [F]
    26 A2
Garlin [F] 36 DE2
Gastes [F] 30 B2
Gaubert [F] 18 D2
Gauville [F] 10 E3
Gavarnie [F] 36 E4
Gavarnie, Cirque de– [F] 36 E4
Gavray [F] 10 B3
Geaune [F] 30 C4
Gedinne [B] 14 A2
Geel [B] 6 B4
Geertruidenberg [NL] 6 B2
Geldrop [NL] 6 C3
Geleen [NL] 6 C4
Gembloux [B] 14 A1
Gémenos [F] 40 E3
Gemert [NL] 6 C3
Gémozac [F] 24 B3
Gemmenich [B] 14 C1
Genappe [B] 14 A1
Gençay [F] 24 E2
Génelard [F] 26 E3
Genillé [F] 18 C4
Genk [B] 6 B4
Genlis [F] 28 B2
Gennep [NL] 6 C3
Gennes [F] 18 A3
Génolhac [F] 32 E4
Gent (Gand) [B] 4 E4
Gentioux [F] 26 A4
Geraardsbergen [B] 4 E4
Gérardmer [F] 22 D3
Gerbéviller [F] 22 C2
Germay [F] 20 E2
Germigny–des–Pres [F] 18 E3
Gespunsart [F] 14 A3
Gévezé [F] 8 E4
Gevigney–et–Mercey [F] 20 F4
Gevrey–Chambertin [F] 28 B2
Gex [F] 28 D4
Ghisonaccia [F] 44 C3
Ghisoni [F] 44 B3
Giat [F] 26 B4
Gien [F] 18 F3
Giens [F] 40 F4
Gieten [NL] 2 E3
Giethoorn [NL] 2 D3
Gignac [F] 40 B2
Gimat [F] 30 E4
Gimel–les–Cascades [F] 32 C1
Gimont [F] 38 A1
Girolata [F] 44 A2
Giromagny [F] 22 C4
Gisors [F] 12 A3
Gistel [B] 4 D3
Givet [F] 14 A2

Givors [F] 34 B2
Givry [B] 12 F1
Givry [F] 26 F2
Givry [F] 20 B4
Givry–en–Argonne [F] 20 E1
Gizeux [F] 18 B3
Glénic [F] 26 B3
Gneux [F] 12 E4
Goderville [F] 10 E2
Goes [NL] 4 E3
Goirle [NL] 6 B3
Golfe–Juan [F] 42 C3
Golfo di Sogno [F] 44 B4
Goncelin [F] 34 D2
Gondrecourt [F] 20 E2
Gondrin [F] 30 D4
Gooik [B] 4 E4
Goor [NL] 2 D4
Gordes [F] 40 E2
Gorinchem [NL] 6 B2
Gorredijk [NL] 2 D2
Gorron [F] 10 C4
Gouarec [F] 8 C3
Gouda [NL] 6 B2
Goules, Col des– [F] 26 C4
Goulven [F] 8 B2
Gourdon [F] 32 B2
Gourin [F] 8 C3
Gournay–en–Bray [F] 12 B2
Gourville [F] 24 D3
Gout–Rossignol [F] 24 D4
Gouvets [F] 10 C3
Gouzon [F] 26 B3
Graçay [F] 18 D4
Gradignan [F] 30 C2
Grainetière, Abbaye de la– [F]
    16 E4
Gramat [F] 32 B2
Grancey–le–Château [F] 20 D4
Grandcamp–Maisy [F] 10 C2
Grand–Champ [F] 16 C1
Grand Chartreuse, Couvent de la–
    [F] 34 D2
Grande–Fougeray [F] 16 D2
Grandjouan [F] 16 D2
Grandpré [F] 14 A4
Grandrieu [F] 32 E3
Grand Roc [F] 30 F2
Grand–Rozoy [F] 12 D3
Grandvilliers [F] 12 B2
Grange–Bleneau, Château de
    la– [F] 20 B1
Grange–le–Bocage [F] 20 B2
Granges–sur–Vologne [F]
    22 D3
Granville [F] 10 B3
Grassac [F] 24 D4
Grasse [F] 42 C3
Graulhet [F] 38 D1
Grave [NL] 6 C2
Gravelines [F] 4 C3
Gray [F] 28 C1
Grayan–et–Hôpital [F] 24 B3
Grenade [F] 30 C4
Grenade [F] 38 C1
Grenoble [F] 34 D2
Gréolières [F] 42 C2
Gréoux–les–Bains [F] 40 F2
Greux [F] 20 F2
Grevenmacher [L] 14 C3
Grez–en–Bouère [F] 16 F2
Grignan [F] 34 B4
Grignols [F] 30 D3
Grimaud [F] 42 B3
Grisolles [F] 32 A4
Groenlo [NL] 6 D2
Groix [F] 16 B1
Groningen [NL] 2 E2
Grostenquin [F] 22 D1
Grouw [NL] 2 D2
Gruissan [F] 38 E3
Guagno [F] 44 B2

Guebwiller [F] 22 D4
Guémené–Penfao [F] 16 D2
Guémené–sur–Scorff [F] 8 C4
Guenange [F] 14 C4
Guer [F] 16 D1
Guérande [F] 16 C2
Guéret [F] 26 A3
Guérigny [F] 26 D1
Guethary [F] 30 A4
Gueugnon [F] 26 E3
Guichen [F] 16 D1
Guignes [F] 20 A1
Guillaumes [F] 42 C2
Guillestre [F] 34 E4
Guilvinec [F] 8 B4
Guimiliau [F] 8 B3
Guînes [F] 4 B3
Guingamp [F] 8 D3
Guipry [F] 16 D1
Guise [F] 12 E2
Guissény [F] 8 B2
Guitalens [F] 38 D1
Gultres [F] 30 D1
Gujan–Mestras [F] 30 B2
Gurgazu [F] 44 B4
Guzet–Neige [F] 38 B3
Gy [F] 28 C1

H

Haaksbergen [NL] 6 E2
Haarlem [NL] 2 B3
Habas [F] 36 CD2
Habay [B] 14 B3
Hagetmau [F] 30 C4
Hagondange [F] 14 C4
Haguenau [F] 22 E2
Hallignicourt [F] 20 D2
Halluin [F] 4 D4
Halsteren [NL] 4 F3
Ham [F] 12 D2
Hambye, Abbaye de– [F] 10 C3
Hamoir [B] 14 B1
Hannuit (Hannut) [B] 14 B1
Hannut (Hannuit) [B] 14 B1
Han–sur–Lesse [B] 14 B2
Han–sur–Nied [F] 22 C1
Haras du Pin [F] 10 E4
Hardelot–Plage [F] 4 B4
Hardenberg [NL] 2 E3
Harderwijk [NL] 2 C4
Haren [NL] 2 E2
Harfleur [F] 10 E2
Hargnies [F] 14 A2
Harlingen [NL] 2 C2
Harmelen [NL] 2 B4
Haroué [F] 22 C2
Hasparren [F] 36 C2
Hasselt [B] 6 B4
Hasselt [NL] 2 D3
Hastiere–Lavaux [B] 14 A2
Hattem [NL] 2 D4
Hattonchâtel [F] 20 F1
Haule [NL] 2 D2
Haut–Asco [F] 44 B2
Haut–Barr, Château du– [F] 22 D2
Hautecombe, Abbaye de– [F] 34 D1
Hautefort, Château de– [F] 32 B1
Hauteville–Lompnes [F] 34 D1
Hauteville Plage [F] 10 B2
Haut Kœnigsbourg [F] 22 D3
Hautmont [F] 12 E1
Havelange [B] 14 B1
Hayange [F] 14 C4

Hazebrouck [F] 4 C4
Hechtel [B] 6 B4
Hédauville [F] 12 C2
Hédé [F] 8 F4
Heemstede [NL] 2 B3
Heerde [NL] 2 D4
Heerenveen [NL] 2 D2
Heeze [NL] 6 C3
Heino [NL] 2 D4
Heippes [F] 22 A1
Hellendoorn [NL] 2 D4
Hellevoetsluis [NL] 4 F2
Helmond [NL] 6 C3
Hèming [F] 22 D2
Hendaye [F] 36 B2
Hendrik Ido Ambacht [NL] 6 B2
Hengelo [NL] 2 E4
Hénin Beaumont [F] 12 D1
Hennebont [F] 16 B1
Hennezel [F] 22 B3
Hénoville [F] 4 B4
Henrichemont [F] 18 E4
Hérault, Gorges de l'– [F] 40 B2
Herbault [F] 18 C3
Herbesthal [B] 14 C1
Herbeumont [B] 14 B3
Herbignac [F] 16 C2
Herentals [B] 6 B3
Héricourt [F] 28 D1
Hérisson [F] 26 C2
Herment [F] 26 B4
Herselt [B] 6 B4
Het Loo [NL] 2 D4
Hettange–Grande [F] 14 C4
Heverlee [B] 6 A4
Heyrieux [F] 34 C2
Hiersac [F] 24 D3
Hillegom [NL] 2 B4
Hillion [F] 8 D3
Hilvarenbeek [NL] 6 B3
Hilversum [NL] 2 B4
Hirsingue [F] 28 E1
Hirson [F] 12 F2
Hochfelden [F] 22 E2
Hoedekenskerke [NL] 4 E3
Hoek van Holland [NL] 2 A4
Hohneck [F] 22 D3
Hohrodberg [F] 22 D3
Hollum [NL] 2 D1
Holten [NL] 2 D4
Holwerd [NL] 2 D2
Homps [F] 38 E2
Honfleur [F] 10 E2
Hoofddorp [NL] 2 B4
Hoogerheide [NL] 4 F3
Hoogeveen [NL] 2 D3
Hoogezand [NL] 2 E2
Hoogkarspel [NL] 2 C3
Hoogstraten [B] 6 B3
Hoorn [NL] 2 B3
Hordain [F] 12 E1
Hornoy [F] 12 B2
Horst [B] 6 A4
Horst [NL] 6 C3
Hoscheid [L] 14 C3
Hospice de France [F] 36 F4
Hossegor [F] 30 A4
Hostens [F] 30 C2
Hotton [B] 14 B2
Houdan [F] 12 A4
Houdelaincourt [F] 20 E2
Houeillès [F] 30 D3
Houffalize [B] 14 C2
Houlgate [F] 10 E2
Hourtin [F] 24 B4
Hourtin–Plage [F] 24 A4
Houthalen [NL] 6 C4
Hucqueliers [F] 4 B4
Huelgoat [F] 8 C3
Huizen [NL] 2 B3

Huizen [NL] 2 C4
Hulst [NL] 4 E3
Hunaudaye, Château de– [F] 8 E3
Hunspach [F] 22 E2
Huriel [F] 26 C3
Huy (Hoei) [B] 14 B1
Hyères [F] 40 F4

I

Ichtratzheim [F] 22 E3
Ieper (Ypres) [B] 4 D4
If, Château d'– [F] 40 E3
IJmuiden [NL] 2 B3
Illiers–Combray [F] 18 D1
Imphy [F] 26 D2
Ingelmunster [B] 4 D4
Ingwiller [F] 22 E2
Isdes [F] 18 E3
Isigni–sur–Mer [F] 10 C2
Isola [F] 42 C2
Isola 2000 [F] 42 C2
Issigeac [F] 30 E2
Issoire [F] 32 E1
Issoudun [F] 26 B1
Is–sur–Tille [F] 20 D4
Istres [F] 40 D3
Isturits et d'Oxocelhaya, Grottes d'– [F] 36 C2
Itxassou [F] 36 C2
Ivry–la–Bataille [F] 12 A4
Izegem [B] 4 D4
Izernore [F] 28 B4

J

Jaligny–sur–Besbre [F] 26 D3
Jarmenil [F] 22 C3
Janville [F] 18 D2
Janvry [F] 18 E1
Janzé [F] 16 E1
Jardin [F] 18 B3
Jard–sur–Mer [F] 24 A1
Jargeau [F] 18 E3
Jarnac [F] 24 C3
Jarnages [F] 26 B3
Jarny [F] 14 B4
Jaubrun [F] 32 D3
Jauge [F] 30 C2
Jausiers [F] 42 C1
Javerdat [F] 24 E3
Javron [F] 10 D4
Jeumont [F] 12 F1
Joigny [F] 20 B3
Joinville [F] 20 E2
Jonas, Grottes de– [F] 32 E1
Joncy [F] 26 F3
Jonzac [F] 24 C4
Josselin [F] 16 C1
Jouarre [F] 12 D4
Jougne [F] 28 D3
Joure [NL] 2 D2
Joyeuse [F] 32 F4
Juan–les–Pins [F] 42 C3
Jugon–les–Lacs [F] 8 E3
Juillac [F] 32 B1
Jullouville [F] 8 F3
Jumièges [F] 10 F2

Juniville [F] 12 F3
Jurignac [F] 24 CD4
Jussey [F] 20 F4
Juvigny–le–Tertre [F] 10 C3
Juzennecourt [F] 20 D3

K

Kaatsheuvel [NL] 6 B2
Kampen [NL] 2 D3
Kamperland [NL] 4 E2
Kasterlee [B] 6 B3
Katwijk aan Zee [NL] 2 A4
Kaysersberg [F] 22 D3
Kerien [F] 8 D3
Kerjean, Château de– [F] 8 B2
Kernascléden [F] 8 C4
Keskastel [F] 22 D1
Kinrooi [B] 6 C4
Kiriou, Roche de– [F] 8 C3
Klazienaveen [NL] 2 E3
Klerken [B] 4 D3
Knokke–Heist [B] 4 D3
Koetschette [L] 14 C3
Koksijde–Bad [B] 4 C3
Korrigans [F] 16 C2
Kortenberg [B] 4 F1
Kortrijk (Courtrai) [B] 4 D4
Kotten [F] 6 E2
Kruiningen [NL] 4 E3
Kruisland [NL] 4 F3

la Balme [F] 34 C3
La Bastide [F] 42 B2
Labastide–d'Armagnac [F] 30 D3
La Bastide de–Sérou [F] 38 C3
Labastide–Murat [F] 32 B3
La Bastide–Puylaurent [F] 32 F3
Labastide–Rouairoux [F] 38 E2
La Bastie d'Urfé [F] 34 A1
La Bâtie–Neuve [F] 34 D4
La Baule [F] 16 C2
La Bazoche–Gouet [F] 18 C2
la Bégude–de–Mazenc [F] 34 B4
La Belle Etoile [F] 20 C2
Labenne [F] 30 A4
La Bérarde [F] 34 E3
L'Aber–Wrac'h [F] 8 B2
Laborel [F] 40 E1
Labouheyre [F] 30 B3
La Bourboule [F] 32 D1
Labrède [F] 30 C2
La Bresse [F] 22 D3
La Brillanne [F] 40 F2
Labrit [F] 30 C3
La Caillere–St–Hilaire [F] 24 C1
Lacalm [F] 32 D3
Lacanau [F] 30 C1
Lacanau–Océan [F] 30 B1
La Canonica [F] 44 C2
La Canourgue [F] 32 D4
La Capelle [F] 12 E2
Lacapelle–Marival [F] 32 B3
La Capte [F] 40 F4
Lacaune [F] 38 E1
La Cavalerie [F] 38 F1

Lacave [F] 32 B2
La Celle–Dunoise [F] 26 A3
La Chaise–Dieu [F] 32 F2
La Chambre [F] 34 E2
Lachamp [F] 32 E3
La Chapelle [F] 26 E2
La Chapelle–d'Angillon [F] 18 E4
la Chapelle–en–Valgaudemar [F] 34 D3
La Chapelle–en–Vercors [F] 34 C3
La Chapelle–Glain [F] 16 E2
la–Chapelle–Laurent [F] 32 E2
La Charité–sur–Loire [F] 26 D1
La Chartre–sur–le–Loir [F] 18 C2
La Châtaigneraie [F] 24 C1
La Châtre [F] 26 B2
La–Chevignerie [F] 16 D2
la Chèze [F] 8 D4
La Ciotat [F] 40 E3
La Clayette [F] 26 E3
la Clisse [F] 24 B3
La Clusaz [F] 34 E1
La Cluse [F] 28 B4
La Cluse–et–Mijoux [F] 28 D3
La Colle Noire [F] 42 C3
La Coquille [F] 24 E4
La Corrèze [F] 32 C2
La Côte–St–André [F] 34 C2
Lacourt [F] 38 B3
La Courtine [F] 26 B4
la Couvertoirade [F] 38 F1
Lacq [F] 36 D2
La Croisière [F] 24 F3
La Croix Ferrée [F] 24 F4
La Croixille [F] 16 E1
La Croix–Valmer [F] 42 B4
La Cure [F] 28 C3
Ladapeyre [F] 26 B3
Ladon [F] 18 F2
Ladoye, Cirque de– [F] 28 C3
La Fère [F] 12 D3
La Ferrière [F] 18 C3
La Ferrière [F] 34 D2
La Ferrière–en–Parthenay [F] 24 D1
Laferté [F] 20 E4
La Ferté–Bernard [F] 18 C2
la–Ferté–Chevresis [F] 12 E2
La Ferté–Gaucher [F] 20 B1
La–Ferté–Loupière [F] 20 B3
La Ferté–Macé [F] 10 D4
La Ferté–Milon [F] 12 D3
La Ferté–sous–Jouarre [F] 12 D4
La Ferté–St–Aubin [F] 18 E3
La Ferté–Vidame [F] 10 F4
La–Feuille [F] 12 B2
Laffrey [F] 34 D3
La Flèche [F] 18 B2
La Flotte [F] 24 B2
Lafrançaise [F] 30 F4
La Gacilly [F] 16 D1
Lagarde [F] 22 C2
La Garde–Freinet [F] 42 B3
L'Agiot Élancourt [F] 12 B4
Lagnieu [F] 34 C1
Lagny [F] 12 C4
La Grand–Combe [F] 32 F4
La Grande–Motte [F] 40 C2
Lagrasse [F] 38 E3
La Grave [F] 34 E3
Laguépie [F] 32 B4
La Guerche–de–Bretagne [F] 16 E1
La Guerche–sur–l'Aubois [F] 26 C2
Laguiole [F] 32 D3
Lahane [F] 30 B3

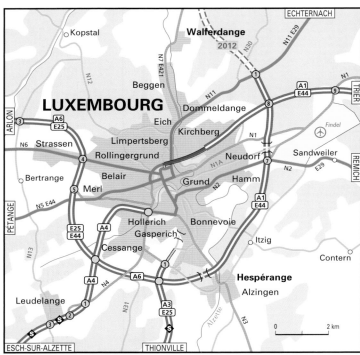

ECHTERNACH

○ Kopstal

Walferdange

2012

N7 E421

N12

N11 E29

N30

Beggen

① N1

TRIER

LUXEMBOURG

A1 E44

⑨

Dommeldange

⑧

Eich

ARLON ③

A6 E25

Kirchberg

N1

Findel

N6 Strassen

Limpertsberg

Rollingergrund

Neudorf

⑦

Sandweiler

④

N1A

N2 E29

REMICH

○ Bertrange

Belair

⑤ Merl

Grund

N2

Hamm

N5 E44

Gasperich

Hollerich

Bonnevoie

Itzig ○

PETANGE

N13

E25 E44

A4

Cessange

①

Contern ○

Leudelange

A4

N31

A6

①

Hespérange

N4

A3 E25

Alzingen

Alzette

N3

0   2 km

ESCH-SUR-ALZETTE   THIONVILLE

Laubrières [F] 16 E1
Laugnac [F] 30 E3
Laugratte [F] 30 E2
Laurière [F] 24 F3
Lauterbourg [F] 22 F2
Lautrec [F] 38 D1
Lauwersoog [NL] 2 D2
Lauzerte [F] 30 F3
Lauzun [F] 30 E2
La Vacherie [F] 34 C3
Laval [F] 16 F1
Lavardac [F] 30 D3
Lavardin [F] 18 C2
Lavaur [F] 38 C1
Lavelanet [F] 38 C3
la Veurdre [F] 26 D2
Lavit [F] 30 E4
La Voulte-sur-Rhône [F] 34 B3
Lavoûte-Chilhac [F] 32 E2
Lavoûte-Polignac, Château de- [F] 32 F2
Lavoûte-sur-Loire [F] 32 F2
Lavoye [F] 20 E1
La Wantzenau [F] 22 E2
Le Ballon [F] 16 E1
Le Bar [F] 42 C3
Le Barp [F] 30 C2
Le Beausset [F] 40 E3
Le Biot [F] 28 D4
Le Blanc [F] 24 F2
Le Boréon [F] 42 C2
Le Boulou [F] 38 E4
Le Bourg d'Oisans [F] 34 D3
Le Bourget [F] 34 D2
Le Bousquet-d'Orb [F] 38 F2
Le Bugue [F] 30 F2
Le Calanche [F] 44 A2
le Caloy [F] 30 C3
Le Cap-d'Agde [F] 38 F3
Le Cateau-Cambrésis [F] 12 E2
Le Catelet [F] 12 D2
Le Caylar [F] 38 F1
L'Echalp [F] 34 F4
Le Chambon-sur-Lignon [F] 34 A3
Le Chateau-d'Oléron [F] 24 B3
Le Châtelard [F] 34 E2
Le Châtelet [F] 26 B2
Le Chesne [F] 14 A3
Le Cheylard [F] 34 B3
Le Conquet [F] 8 A3
Le Coteau [F] 26 E4
Le Creusot [F] 26 F2
Le Croisic [F] 16 C2
Le Crotoy [F] 12 B1
Lectoure [F] 30 E4
Lédignan [F] 40 C1
Le Donjon [F] 26 E3
Le Dorat [F] 24 F3
Leek [NL] 2 D2
Leens [NL] 2 D2
Leerdam [NL] 6 B2
Leeuwarden [NL] 2 D2
Le Faou [F] 8 B3
Le Faouët [F] 8 C4
le Fayet [F] 34 E1
le Folgoet [F] 8 B2
Le Fossat [F] 38 C2
Le Freney [F] 34 E3
le Fuilet [F] 16 E3
le-Gault-St-Denis [F] 18 D2
Legé [F] 16 D3
le Gouray [F] 8 E3
Le Grand-Bourg [F] 26 A3
Le Grand-Lucé [F] 18 C2
Le Grand-Pressigny [F] 18 C4
Le Grau-du-Roi [F] 40 C2
Le Gressier [F] 30 B1
Léguevin [F] 38 B1
Le Havre [F] 10 E2

la Haye [F] 12 A2
La Haye-du-Puits [F] 10 B2
Laheycourt [F] 20 E1
La Hutte [F] 18 B1
Laifour, Roches de- [F] 14 A2
L'Aigle [F] 10 E4
Laignes [F] 20 C3
L'Aiguillon [F] 24 B2
Laissac [F] 32 D4
Laize-la-Ville [F] 10 D3
la-Jaille-Yvon [F] 16 F2
La Javie [F] 42 B2
la Jonchère-St-Maurice [F] 24 F3
Lalinde [F] 30 E2
La Loupe [F] 18 D1
Lalouvesc [F] 34 B2
La Louvière [B] 12 F1
L'Alpe-d'Huez [F] 34 D3
La Machine [F] 26 D2
La Malène [F] 32 E4
Lamalou-les-Bains [F] 38 F2
Lamarche [F] 20 E3
Lamargelle [F] 20 D4
Lamarque [F] 30 C1
Lamastre [F] 34 B3
La Maucarrière [F] 16 F4
Lamballe [F] 8 E3
Lambesc [F] 40 E2
la-Melleraye-de-Bretagne [F] 16 E2
Le Mongie [F] 36 E3
La Mothe-Achard [F] 16 D4
La-Mothe-St-Héray [F] 24 D2
Lamotte-Beuvron [F] 18 E3
La Motte-Chalancon [F] 34 C4

la Motte-du-Caire [F] 40 F1
Lamouroux, Grottes de- [F] 32 B2
Lampaul [F] 8 A2
Lampaul-Plouarzel [F] 8 A2
La Mure [F] 34 D3
Lamure-sur-Azergues [F] 26 F4
La Napoule-Plage [F] 42 C3
Landépéreuse [F] 10 E3
Landerneau [F] 8 B3
Landévennec [F] 8 B3
Landivisiau [F] 8 B3
Landivy [F] 10 C4
Landrecies [F] 12 E2
Landudec [F] 8 B4
Le Neuve-Lyre [F] 10 F3
Langeac [F] 32 E2
Langeais [F] 18 B3
Langogne [F] 32 F3
Langoiran [F] 30 D1
Langon [F] 30 D2
Langres [F] 20 E3
Languidou, Chapelle de- [F] 8 B4
Lanleff, Temple de- [F] 8 D3
Lanmeur [F] 8 C2
Lannemezan [F] 36 E3
Lannilis [F] 8 B2
Lannion [F] 8 C2
Lanobre [F] 32 D1
Lanouaille [F] 30 F1
Lanslebourg-Mont-Cenis [F] 34 F3
Lantosque [F] 42 C2
Lanvollon [F] 8 D3
Laon [F] 12 E3

La Pacaudière [F] 26 E3
Lapalisse [F] 26 D3
La Pallice [F] 24 B2
Lapalme [F] 38 E3
La Palud-sur-Verdon [F] 42 B2
La Panouse [F] 32 E3
la Péruse [F] 24 E3
La Petite-Pierre [F] 22 D2
Lapeyrade [F] 30 D3
La Plagne [F] 34 E2
La Plaine-Sur-Mer [F] 16 C3
Laplume [F] 30 E3
Lapoutroie [F] 22 D3
La Primaude [F] 32 C4
Laqueuille [F] 32 D1
Laragne-Montéglin [F] 40 F1
l'Arbre [F] 24 D3
L'Arbresle [F] 34 B1
Larceveau-Arros-Cibits [F] 36 C2
Larche [F] 32 B2
Larche [F] 42 C1
La Réole [F] 30 D2
Largentière [F] 34 A4
L'Argentière-la-Bessée [F] 34 E4
L'Armelliere [F] 40 D2
Larmor [F] 16 B1
La Roche-Bernard [F] 16 C2
La Roche-Chalais [F] 30 D1
la Roche-de-Rame [F] 34 E4
la Roche-Derrien [F] 8 D2
La Roche-en-Ardenne [B] 14 B2
La Rochefoucauld [F] 24 D3
La Rochelle [F] 24 B2

La Roche-Posay [F] 24 E1
La Roche-sur-Foron [F] 28 C4
La Roche-sur-Yon [F] 16 D4
La Rochette [F] 34 D2
Larochette [L] 14 C3
Laroquebrou [F] 32 C2
La Roquebrussanne [F] 40 F3
Laroque-des-Arcs [F] 32 B3
Laroque-d'Olmes [F] 38 C3
La Roque-Gageac [F] 30 F2
La Rouche-Courbon [F] 24 B3
Larrau [F] 36 C3
Larret [F] 20 E4
Larroque [F] 32 B4
l'Artigue [F] 38 B3
Laruns [F] 36 D3
la Salles-les Alpes [F] 34 E3
La Salvetat [F] 32 C4
La Salvetat-sur-Agout [F] 38 E2
Lascaux, Grotte de- [F] 32 A2
la Selve [F] 32 C4
La Seyne [F] 40 E4
La Souterraine [F] 24 F3
Lassay [F] 10 C4
Lassigny [F] 12 D3
La Suze-sur-Sarthe [F] 18 B2
La Tannière [F] 10 C4
La Tour-du-Pin [F] 34 C2
La Tranche-sur-Mer [F] 24 B1
Latresne [F] 30 CD2
La Trimouille [F] 24 F2
La Trinité [F] 16 B1
La Trinité-Porhoët [F] 8 D4
Latronquière [F] 32 C2
Latte, Fort la- [F] 8 E3
La Turbie [F] 42 D3

Le–Hérie–La Vieville [F] 12 E2
Le Hohwald [F] 22 D3
Le Houga [F] 30 C4
Leiden [NL] 2 A4
Le Lauzet–Ubaye [F] 42 B1
Le Lavandou [F] 42 B4
le Liège [F] 18 C4
Le Lion–d'Angers [F] 16 F2
Le Logis–du–Pin [F] 42 B2
Le Loroux–Bottereau [F] 16 E3
Le Louroux [F] 16 E2
Le Luc [F] 42 B3
Le Ludd [F] 18 B2
Lelystad [NL] 2 C3
Le Mans [F] 18 B2
Le Markstein [F] 22 D4
Le Mas–d'Azil [F] 38 B2
Le Mayet [F] 26 D3
Lembach [F] 22 E1
Lembeye [F] 16 E2
Lemele [NL] 2 D4
Le Merlerault [F] 10 E4
Le–Mesnil–Vigot [F] 10 C2
Lemmer [NL] 2 C3
Le Monastier [F] 32 F3
Le Monêtier–les–Bains [F]
    34 E3
Le Mont–Dore [F] 32 D1
Le Monteix [F] 32 D1
Le Montet [F] 26 C3
Le Mont–St–Michel [F] 8 F3
Le Moulin du Pali [F] 42 C2
Lempdes [F] 26 C4
Lempdes [F] 32 E2
le Mulins [F] 26 E4
Le Muret [F] 30 C2
Le Muy [F] 42 B3
Lenclôitre [F] 24 E1
Lencouacq [F] 30 C3
Le Neubourg [F] 10 F3
Léning [F] 22 D1
Le Nouvion–en–Thiérache [F]
    12 E2
Lens [F] 12 D1
Léon [F] 30 B3
Leopoldsburg [B] 6 B4
Le Palais [F] 16 B2
Le Palmyre [F] 24 B3
L'Epau, Abbaye de– [F] 18 B2
Le–Péage–de–Roussillon [F]
    34 B2
Le Perthus [F] 38 E4
Le Pin–au–Haras [F] 10 E4
l'Epine [F] 20 D1
Le Pleynet [F] 34 D3
Le Poiré–sur–Vie [F] 16 D4
Le Pont [F] 34 D2
Le Pont–de–Beauvoisin [F]
    34 D2
Le Pont–de–Claix [F] 34 D3
le Pont–de–Montvert [F] 32 E4
Le Pontet [F] 24 B4
le Porge [F] 30 BC1
Le Pouldu [F] 16 B1
Le Pouzin [F] 34 B3
Le Puy–en–Velay [F] 32 F2
Leques, Col des– [F] 42 B2
Le Quesnoy [F] 12 E1
Le Rabot [F] 18 E3
Lerm–et–Musset [F] 30 D3
Le Rozier [F] 32 D4
Le Russey [F] 28 D2
Les Abrets [F] 34 C3
Les Adrets [F] 42 C3
Les Aix–d'Angillon [F] 18 E4
les Aldudes [F] 36 B2
Les Andelys [F] 12 A3
Les Antiques [F] 40 D2
Les Arcs [F] 34 F2
Les Arcs [F] 42 B3
Les Baux–de–Provence [F]
    40 D2

Les Bouchoux [F] 28 C4
Les Boulay Lue [F] 22 C1
Les Cabannes [F] 38 C3
Les Calanques [F] 40 E3
Lescar [F] 36 D2
L'Escarène [F] 42 D2
Les Contamines–Montjoie [F]
    34 E1
Les Deux–Alpes [F] 34 D3
Lesdins [F] 12 D2
Les Echarmeaux [F] 26 E4
Les Echelles [F] 34 D2
Les Epesses [F] 16 E4
Les Eyzies–de–Tayac [F] 30 F2
Les–Fins [F] 28 D2
Les Forges [F] 8 D4
Les Gets [F] 28 D4
Les Halles [F] 34 B1
Les Hayons [F] 12 A2
Les Herbiers [F] 16 E4
Les Houches [F] 34 F1
Les Issambres [F] 42 B3
Les Laumes [F] 20 C4
Les Lecques [F] 40 E3
Les Menuires [F] 34 E2
Lesmont [F] 20 D2
Lesneven [F] 8 B2
Lesparre–Médoc [F] 24 B4
Lesperon [F] 30 B3
Les Pieux [F] 10 B1
Les Planches–en–Montagne [F]
    28 C3
Les Ponts–de–Cé [F] 16 F3
Les Riceys [F] 20 C3
Les Rosiers [F] 18 A3
Les Rousses [F] 28 C3
Les Sables–d'Olonne [F] 16 C4
Les Saisies [F] 34 E2
Les Salles [F] 26 D4
Lessay [F] 10 B2
Lestards [F] 32 C1
Lestelle Bétharram [F] 36 D3
Les–Thilliers–en–Vexin [F]
    12 B3
Les Trois–Epis [F] 22 D3
Les Trois–Moutiers [F] 18 A4
Les Vans [F] 32 F4
Le Teil [F] 34 B4
Le Teilleul [F] 10 C4
le Temple [F] 30 C1
Le Thillot [F] 22 C4
Le Touquet–Paris–Plage [F]
    4 B4
Le Touvet [F] 34 D2
Le Trayas [F] 42 C3
Le Tremblade [F] 24 B3
Le Tréport [F] 12 B1
Leucate [F] 38 E3
Leuglay [F] 20 D3
Leuven (Louvain) [B] 6 A4
Le Val–André [F] 8 E3
le Vast [F] 10 C1
Le Vaudreuil [F] 12 A3
Levens [F] 42 C2
Le Verdon [F] 24 B3
Le Vernet [F] 42 B1
Levet [F] 26 C2
Levie [F] 44 B3
Levier [F] 28 C2
Le Vigan [F] 40 B1
Levroux [F] 26 A1
Lézardrieux [F] 8 D2
Lézat [F] 28 C3
Lezay [F] 24 D2
Lézignan–Corbières [F] 38 E3
Lezoux [F] 26 D4
l'Hermitage–Lorge [F] 8 D3
l'Hospitalet–l'Andorre [F]
    38 C3
Libourne [F] 30 D1
Libramont [B] 14 B2
Lichtenberg [F] 22 E2

Lichtenvoorde [NL] 6 D2
Licques [F] 4 B4
Liège (Luik) [B] 14 B1
Lier [B] 4 F4
Liernais [F] 26 F1
Lierville [F] 12 B3
Liesse [F] 12 E3
Lieu–Restauré, Abbaye de– [F]
    12 D3
Lieurey [F] 10 E3
Liffré [F] 8 F4
Ligneuville [B] 14 C2
Lignières [F] 26 B2
Ligny–en–Barrois [F] 20 E2
Ligueil [F] 18 C4
Ligugé, Abbaye de– [F] 24 D2
L'Ile–Bouchard [F] 18 B4
L'Ile–Rousse [F] 44 B1
Lillebonne [F] 10 F2
Limbourg [B] 14 C1
Limoges [F] 24 F3
Limogne–en–Quercy [F] 32 B3
Limonest [F] 34 B1
Limours [F] 18 E1
Limoux [F] 38 D3
Lipsheim [F] 22 E3
Lisieux [F] 10 E3
Lisle [F] 30 E1
L'Isle–Adam [F] 12 B3
L'Isle–de–Noé [F] 36 F2
L'Isle–en–Dodon [F] 38 B2
L'Isle–Jourdain [F] 38 B1
L'Isle–sur–la–Sorgue [F] 40 D2
L'Isle–sur–le–Doubs [F] 28 D1
Lisle–sur–Tarn [F] 38 D1
Lison, Source du– [F] 28 C2
Lisse [NL] 2 B4
Lissewege [B] 4 D3
Lit–et–Mixe [F] 30 B3
Livarot [F] 10 E3
Livernon [F] 32 B3
Livron–sur–Drôme [F] 34 B3
Lizy [F] 12 D4
Llivia [F] 38 C4
Lochem [NL] 6 D2
Loches [F] 18 C4
Locmaria [F] 16 B2
Locmariaquer [F] 16 B2
Locminé [F] 16 C1
Locquirec [F] 8 C2
Locronan [F] 8 B3
Loctudy [F] 8 B4
Lodève [F] 38 F2
Lohéac [F] 16 D1
Loire, Gorges de la– [F] 32 F3
Loisirs, Parc de– [F] 30 B2
Lokeren [B] 4 E3
Lombez [F] 38 B1
Lombrives, Grotte de– [F]
    38 C3
Lomme [F] 4 D4
Lommel [B] 6 B3
Londinières [F] 12 B2
Longeau [F] 20 E4
Longeville les St. Avold [F]
    22 C1
Longny–au–Perche [F] 10 E4
Longpont [F] 12 D3
Longré [F] 24 D3
Longué [F] 18 A3
Longueau [F] 12 C2
Longuyon [F] 14 B3
Longwy [F] 14 B3
Lons–le–Saunier [F] 28 B3
Looberghe [F] 4 C3
Loon Plage [F] 4 C3
Loqueffret [F] 8 C3
Lorcé [B] 14 C1
Lorentzen [F] 22 D1
Lorgues [F] 42 B3
Lorient [F] 16 B1
Loriol–sur–Drôme [F] 34 B3

Lorlanges [F] 32 E2
Lormes [F] 26 E1
Lormont [F] 30 C1
Lorris [F] 18 F3
l'Ospedale [F] 44 B4
Losse [F] 30 D3
Loubens–Lauragais [F] 38 C1
Loudéac [F] 8 D4
Loudes [F] 32 F2
Loudun [F] 18 A4
Loué [F] 18 B2
Loue, Source de la– [F] 28 D2
Louhans [F] 28 B3
Loulay [F] 24 C2
Louppy–sur–Loison [F] 14 B3
Lourdes [F] 36 E3
Loury [F] 18 E2
Louvain (Leuven) [B] 6 A4
Louvie–Juzon [F] 36 D3
Louviers [F] 12 A3
Louvigné–du–Desert [F]
    10 BC4
Lozari [F] 44 B1
Lubersac [F] 32 B1
Lucenay [F] 26 F2
Luc–en–Diois [F] 34 C4
Luçon [F] 24 B1
Luc–sur–Mer [F] 10 D2
Luigny [F] 18 D1
Luik (Liège) [B] 14 B1
Lumbres [F] 4 B4
Lummen [B] 6 B4
Lunas [F] 38 F2
Lunel [F] 40 C2
Lunéville [F] 22 C2
Lunteren [NL] 2 C4
Lupiac [F] 30 D4
Lurcy–Lévis [F] 26 C2
Lure [F] 22 C4
Lureuil [F] 24 F1
Luri [F] 44 C1
Lusignan [F] 24 D2
Lusigny [F] 20 C2
Lus–la–Croix–Haute [F] 34 D4
Lussac–les–Châteaux [F]
    24 E2
Lussac–les–Églises [F] 24 F2
Lussan [F] 40 C1
Lux [F] 28 A2
Luxembourg [L] 14 C3
Luxeuil–les–Bains [F] 22 C4
Luxey [F] 30 C3
Luzarches [F] 12 C3
Luzeret [F] 24 F2
Luz–St–Sauveur [F] 36 E3
Luzy [F] 26 E2
Lyon [F] 34 C1
Lyons–la–Forêt [F] 12 A3

M

Maasbree [NL] 6 C3
Maaseik [B] 6 C4
Maasland [NL] 4 F2
Maasmechelen [B] 6 C4
Maassluis [NL] 4 F2
Machault [F] 12 F3
Mâchecourt [F] 16 D3
Macinaggio [F] 44 C1
Mâcon [F] 26 F3
Made [NL] 6 B2
Madieres [F] 40 B2
Magescq [F] 30 B3
Magnac–Laval [F] 24 F3
Magneux Hte Rive [F] 34 A1
Magnières [F] 22 C2
Magny–Cours [F] 26 D2

Magny–en–Vexin [F] 12 B3
Magny–Jobert [F] 22 C4
Maguelone [F] 40 B2
Maîche [F] 28 D2
Maillezais [F] 24 C2
Mailly–le–Camp [F] 20 C1
Mailly–la–Chateau [F] 20 B4
Maintenon [F] 18 D1
Maison–Neuve [F] 20 D2
Malaucène [F] 40 E1
Malbouzon [F] 32 D3
Malbuisson [F] 28 D3
Maldegem [B] 4 E3
Malesherbes [F] 18 F2
Malestroit [F] 16 C1
Malfourat, Mine de– [F] 30 E2
Malicorne [F] 18 B2
Malines (Mechelen) [B] 4 F4
Malmédy [B] 14 C2
Malo–les–Bains [F] 4 C3
Maltat [F] 26 E2
Mamers [F] 18 C1
Mancier [F] 30 D4
Mandelieu [F] 42 C3
Mano [F] 30 C2
Manosque [F] 40 E2
Mansle [F] 24 D3
Manso [F] 44 B2
Mantes [F] 12 B3
Manzat [F] 26 C4
Marans [F] 24 B2
Marboz [F] 28 B3
Marcenais [F] 30 D1
Marchaux [F] 28 C2
Marche–en–Famenne [B]
    14 B2
Marcheprime [F] 30 C2
Marciac [F] 36 E2
Marcigny [F] 26 E3
Marcillac–Vallon [F] 32 C3
Marcillat–en–Combraille [F]
    26 C3
Marcilly–le–Hayer [F] 20 B2
Marckolsheim [F] 22 E3
Mardie [F] 18 E3
Marennes [F] 24 B3
Mareuil [F] 24 B1
Mareuil [F] 24 C4
Marhet [B] 14 B2
Mariémont [B] 12 F1
Marieux [F] 12 C1
Marignane [F] 40 D3
Marigny–le–Châtel [F] 20 C2
Marine de Sisco [F] 44 C1
Marines [F] 12 B3
Maringues [F] 26 C4
Marke [B] 4 D4
Marle [F] 12 E2
Marlenheim [F] 22 E2
Marlens [F] 34 E1
Marmande [F] 30 D2
Marmoutier [F] 22 D2
Marnay [F] 28 C2
Marquion [F] 12 D1
Marquise [F] 4 B3
Marseillan [F] 38 F2
Marseillan–Plage [F] 38 F3
Marseille [F] 40 E3
Marseille–en–Beauvaisis [F]
    12 B2
Martel [F] 32 B2
Martelange [B] 14 B3
Marthille [F] 22 C1
Marthon [F] 24 D4
Martigné–Ferchuad [F] 16 E2
Martigues [F] 40 D3
Marvejols [F] 32 E3
Mas d'Azil, Grotte du– [F]
    38 B2
Masevaux [F] 22 D4
Massat [F] 38 B3
Massay [F] 18 D4

Masseret [F] 24 F4
Masseube [F] 36 F2
Massiac [F] 32 E2
Mas Thibert [F] 40 D2
Matha [F] 24 C3
Mathay [F] 28 D1
Matignon [F] 8 E3
Matour [F] 26 F3
Maubeuge [F] 12 E1
Maubourguet [F] 36 E2
Mauléon [F] 16 E4
Mauléon-Licharre [F] 36 C2
Maulévrier [F] 16 E3
Maupas, Château de– [F]
 18 E4
Maupertus-sur-Mer [F] 10 C1
Maure [F] 16 D1
Mauriac [F] 32 C2
Mauron [F] 8 E4
Maurs [F] 32 C3
Maury [F] 38 D3
Mauvezin [F] 38 B1
Mauzé-sur-le-Mignon [F]
 24 C2
Mayenne [F] 10 C4
Mayet [F] 18 B2
Mazagran [F] 12 F3
Mazamet [F] 38 D2
Mazères [F] 38 C2
Mazerulles [F] 22 C2
Méandre de Queuille [F] 26 C4
Meaux [F] 12 C4
Mechelen (Malines) [B] 4 F4
Medemblik [NL] 2 C3
Médous, Grotte de– [F] 36 E3
Meerkerk [NL] 6 B2
Meeuwen [B] 6 C4
Megève [F] 34 E1
Mehun-sur-Yèvre [F] 18 E4
Meijel [NL] 6 C3
Meillant, Château de– [F]
 26 C2
Meilleraye, Abbaye de– [F]
 16 E2
Mélisey [F] 22 C4
Melle [F] 24 D2
Melrand [F] 8 C4
Melun [F] 18 F1
Menat [F] 26 C3
Mende [F] 32 E3
Menec [F] 16 B1
Menen [B] 4 D4
Ménez Hom [F] 8 B3
Ménigoute [F] 24 D2
Mens [F] 34 D3
Menthon [F] 34 E1
Menton [F] 42 D3
Meppel [NL] 2 D3
Mer [F] 18 D3
Merdrignac [F] 8 E4
Méréville [F] 18 E2
Méribel-les-Allues [F] 34 E2
Merle, Tours de– [F] 32 C2
Merlevenez [F] 16 B1
Mersch [L] 14 C3
Méru [F] 12 B3
Mervans [F] 28 B2
Merville [F] 4 C4
Méry [F] 20 C2
Meschers-sur-Gironde [F]
 24 B3
Meslay [F] 16 F2
Mesnil-Val [F] 12 B1
Messancy [B] 14 B3
Messas [F] 18 D2
Mesvres [F] 26 E2
Metabief [F] 28 D3
Méteren [F] 4 C4
Mettet [B] 14 A1
Metz [F] 22 C1
Metzervisse [F] 14 C4
Meulan [F] 12 B3

Meung-sur-Loire [F] 18 D3
Meux [B] 14 A1
Meximieux [F] 34 C1
Meylan [F] 34 D3
Meymac [F] 32 C1
Meyrargues [F] 40 E2
Meyrueis [F] 32 E4
Meyzieu [F] 34 C1
Mèze [F] 40 B2
Mézel [F] 42 B2
Mézières [F] 24 E3
Mézières-en-Brenne [F] 24 F1
Mézilhac [F] 34 A3
Mézin [F] 30 D3
Mèzos [F] 30 B3
Middelburg [NL] 4 E3
Middelharnis [NL] 4 F2
Middelkerke-Bad [B] 4 D3
Midsland [NL] 2 C1
Miélan [F] 36 E2
Mieussy [F] 28 D4
Migennes [F] 20 B3
Migne [F] 26 A2
Mijoux [F] 28 C4
Millas [F] 38 D4
Millau [F] 32 E4
Millevaches [F] 26 B4
Mimizan [F] 30 B3
Mimizan-Plage [F] 30 B3
Mindin [F] 16 C2
Minervio [F] 44 C1
Minot [F] 20 D4
Miramar [F] 42 C3
Miramas [F] 40 D2
Mirambeau [F] 24 B4
Miramont-de-Guyenne [F]
 30 E2
Mirande [F] 36 F2
Mirebeau [F] 24 D1
Mirebeau [F] 28 B1
Mirecourt [F] 22 B3
Mirepoix [F] 38 C2
Modane [F] 34 E3
Modave [B] 14 B1
Moirans [F] 34 C2
Moirans-en-Montagne [F]
 28 B3
Moissac [F] 30 F4
Mol [B] 6 B3
Molens Van Kinderdijk [NL] 6 B2
Molières [F] 30 F4
Moliets-et-Maa [F] 30 AB3
Molliens [F] 12 B2
Moloy [F] 20 D4
Molsheim [F] 22 E2
Moltifao [F] 44 B2
Moltolieu [F] 38 D2
Monaco [MC] 42 D3
Moncontour [F] 8 D3
Moncoutant [F] 16 E4
Mondaye, Abbaye de– [F] 10 D2
Mondorf-les-Bains [L] 14 C4
Mondoubleau [F] 18 C2
Monestier-de-Clermont [F]
 34 C3
Monêtier-Allemont [F] 40 F1
Monflanquin [F] 30 E3
Monistrol-d'Allier [F] 32 E2
Monistrol-sur-Loire [F] 34 A2
Monnai [F] 10 E3
Monnickendam [NL] 2 B3
Monpazier [F] 30 F2
Monplaisir [F] 18 C2
Mons (Bergen) [B] 12 F1
Monségur [F] 30 D2
Montagnac [F] 38 F2
Montagny [F] 26 E4
Montaigu [F] 16 D3
Montaigu-de-Quercy [F] 30 F3
Montaigut [F] 26 C3
Montaigut-sur-Save [F]
 38 BC1

Montalieu [F] 34 C1
Montalivet-les-Bains [F]
 24 B4
Montaren [F] 40 C1
Montargis [F] 18 F3
Montastruc la–Conseillère [F]
 38 C1
Montauban [F] 8 E4
Montauban [F] 30 F4
Montauriol [F] 38 C1
Montbard [F] 20 C4
Montbazens [F] 32 C3
Montbazon [F] 18 C3
Montbéliard [F] 28 D1
Montbenoît [F] 28 D2
Montbonnot [F] 34 D3
Montbrison [F] 34 A1
Montbron [F] 24 D4
Montbrun-les-Bains [F] 40 E1
Montceau-les-Mines [F]
 26 E2
Montchanin [F] 26 F2
Montcornet [F] 12 E3
Montcuq [F] 30 F3
Mont-de-Marsan [F] 30 C3
Mont-Dol [F] 8 F3
Montebourg [F] 10 C2
Montech [F] 30 F4
Monteil [F] 34 B3
Montel-de-Gelat [F] 26 B4
Montélimar [F] 34 B4
Montendre [F] 24 C4
Montereau [F] 18 F3
Montereau-Faut-Yonne [F]
 20 B2
Montesquieu-Volvestre [F]
 38 B2
Montesquiou [F] 36 F2
Montfaucon-en-Velay [F] 34 A2
Montferrat [F] 42 B3
Montfort [F] 8 E4
Montfort [F] 30 E4
Montfort-en-Chalosse [F]
 30 B4
Montfort l'Amaury [F] 12 B4
Mont Gargan [F] 24 F4
Montgenèvre [F] 34 E3
Montgeoffroy, Château de– [F]
 18 A3
Montgesoye [F] 28 C2
Montgiscard [F] 38 C2
Montguyon [F] 30 D1
Monthermé [F] 14 A2
Monthureux-sur-Saône [F]
 20 F3
Montier-en-Der [F] 20 D2
Montignac [F] 32 A2
Montigny-le-Roi [F] 20 E3
Montigny-sur-Aube [F]
 20 D3
Montivilliers [F] 10 E2
Montlieu-la-Garde [F] 24 C4
Mont-Louis [F] 38 C4
Montluçon [F] 26 C3
Montluel [F] 34 C1
Montmajour, Abbaye de– [F]
 40 D2
Montmarault [F] 26 C3
Montmédy [F] 14 B3
Montmélian [F] 34 D2
Montmeyan [F] 40 F3
Montmirail [F] 18 C2
Montmirail [F] 20 C1
Montmirey [F] 28 B2
Montmoreau-St-Cybard [F]
 24 D4
Montmorillon [F] 24 E2
Montmort [F] 12 E4
Montoire-sur-le-Loir [F]
 18 C2

Montoy-Flanville [F] 22 C1
Montpellier [F] 40 B2
Montpellier-le-Vieux [F]
 32 D4
Montpezat-de-Quercy [F]
 32 B3
Montpon-Ménestérol [F] 30 E1
Montpont-en-Bresse [F] 28 B3
Montréal [F] 20 C4
Montréal [F] 30 D4
Montréal [F] 38 D2
Montredon-Labessonnie [F]
 38 D1
Montréjeau [F] 36 F3
Montrésor [F] 18 C4
Montret [F] 28 B3
Montreuil-aux-Lions [F]
 12 D4
Montreuil-Bellay [F] 18 A3
Montrevault [F] 16 E3
Montrevel-en-Bresse [F]
 28 B3
Montrichard [F] 18 C3
Montrond-les-Bains [F] 34 B1
Montsalvy [F] 32 C3
Montsauche-les-Settons [F]
 26 E1
Montségur [F] 38 C3
Montsoreau [F] 18 B3
Mont-sous-Vaudrey [F] 28 B2
Monts-s-Guesnes [F] 18 B4
Mont-Ste-Odile [F] 22 D3
Montsûrs [F] 18 A1
Monze [F] 38 D3
Moon-sur-Elle [F] 10 C2
Morcenx [F] 30 B3
Mordelles [F] 16 D1
Moreno, Col de la– [F] 26 C4
Morestel [F] 34 C2
Moret-sur-Loing [F] 20 A2
Moreuil [F] 12 C2
Morez [F] 28 C3
Morgat [F] 8 B3
Morgny [F] 12 B3
Morhange [F] 22 C1
Moriani-Plage [F] 44 C2
Morigny Champigny [F]
 18 E1
Moriville [F] 22 C3
Morlaàs [F] 36 D2
Morlaix [F] 8 C3
Mormant [F] 20 A1
Mornay-Berry [F] 26 C1
Morosaglia [F] 44 C2
Mortagne-au-Perche [F]
 10 E4
Mortagne-sur-Sèvre [F]
 16 E3
Mortain [F] 10 C3
Morteau [F] 28 D2
Mortier-Crolle, Château de– [F]
 16 F2
Mortrée [F] 10 D4
Morzine [F] 28 D4
Motricoux [F] 32 B4
Motte-Glain, Château de la– [F]
 16 F2
Mouchard [F] 28 C2
Mougins [F] 42 C3
Moulherne [F] 18 B3
Moulins [F] 26 D2
Moulins-Engilbert [F]
 26 E2
Moulins-la-Marche [F]
 10 E4
Moulismes [F] 24 E2
Moult [F] 10 D3
Moustey [F] 30 C2
Moustiers-Ste-Marie [F]
 42 B2
Mouthe [F] 28 C3
Mouthier [F] 28 D2

Mouthoumet [F] 38 D3
Moutier-d'Ahun [F] 26 B3
Moutiers [F] 24 B1
Moûtiers [F] 34 E2
Mouton-Rothschild [F]
 24 B4
Mouy [F] 12 C3
Mouzon [F] 14 A3

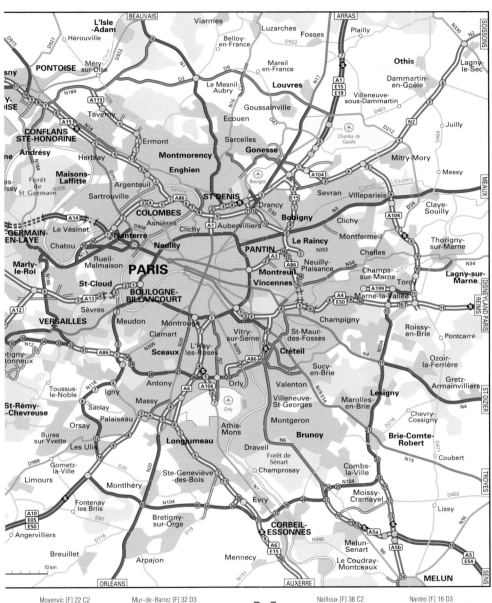

Moyenvic [F] 22 C2
Mt–Dauphin [F] 34 E4
Mugron [F] 30 C4
Mulhouse [F] 22 D4
Munster [F] 22 D3
Murat [F] 32 D2
Murato [F] 44 C2
Murat-sur–Vèbre [F] 38 E2

Mur-de–Barrez [F] 32 D3
Mur-de–Bretagne [F] 8 D4
Muret [F] 38 C2
Muro [F] 44 B2
Musselkanaal [NL] 2 E3
Mussidan [F] 30 E1
Mussy [F] 20 D3
Muzillac [F] 16 C2

Naarden [NL] 2 B4
Nadrin [B] 14 B2

Nailloux [F] 38 C2
Najac [F] 32 B4
Nalzen [F] 38 C3
Namur (Namen) [B] 14 A1
Nancy [F] 22 C2
Nangis [F] 20 B1
Nans-les-Pins [F] 40 E3
Nant [F] 38 F1

Nantes [F] 16 D3
Nanteuil–le-Haudouin [F]
   12 C3
Nantiat [F] 24 F3
Narbonne [F] 38 E3
Narbonne–Plage [F] 38 E3
Nasbinals [F] 32 D3

Naucelle [F] 32 C4
Navacelles, Cirque de– [F]
40 B1
Navarrenx [F] 36 D2
Navilly [F] 28 B2
N.D. de Clausis [F] 34 F4
N.–D. de Kerdevot [F] 8 B4
N.–D. de la Salette [F] 34 D3
N.–D. de Lure [F] 40 F2
N.D. de Miracles [F] 42 C2
N.–D.–du-Haut [F] 22 C4
N.–D. du Mai [F] 40 E4
Neede [NL] 6 D2
Neeroeteren [B] 6 C4
Nedde [F] 26 A4
Négrondes [F] 30 F1
Nemours [F] 18 F2
Nérac [F] 30 D3
Néré [F] 24 C3
Néris–les–Bains [F] 26 C3
Nes [NL] 2 D1
Nesle [F] 12 D2
Nettancourt [F] 20 E1
Neuf–Brisach [F] 22 E4
Neufchâteau [NL] 14 B3
Neufchâteau [F] 20 F2
Neufchâtel–en–Bray [F] 12 B2
Neufchâtel–sur–Aisne [F]
12 E3
Neuillé Port-Pierre [F] 18 B3
Neuilly–l'Évêque [F] 20 E3
Neuilly–St–Front [F] 12 D4
Neu-Moresnet [B] 14 C1
Neung–sur–Beuvron [F] 18 D3
Neuvéglise [F] 32 D2
Neuves–Maisons [F] 22 C2
Neuvic [F] 32 C1
Neuville [F] 24 D1
Neuville [F] 34 C1
Neuville–aux–Bois [F] 18 E2
Neuvilly–en–Argonne [F]
14 A4
Neuvy [F] 26 B2
Neuvy–Bouin [F] 24 C1
Neuvy–sur–Barangeon [F]
18 E4
Nevers [F] 26 D2
Nexon [F] 24 E4
Niaux, Grotte de– [F] 38 C3
Nice [F] 42 C3
Nideck, Château du– [F] 22 D2
Niederbronn–les–Bains [F]
22 E2
Nieppe [F] 4 D4
Nieuil [F] 24 D3
Nieuweschans [NL] 2 F2
Nieuwpoort [B] 4 D3
Nijkerk [NL] 2 C4
Nijmegen [NL] 6 C2
Nijverdal [NL] 2 D4
Nîmes [F] 40 C2
Ninove [B] 4 E4
Niort [F] 24 C2
Nitry [F] 20 C3
Nivelles [B] 12 F1
Niversac [F] 30 F1
Nizy–le–Comte [F] 12 E3
Noailles [F] 12 C3
Nods [F] 28 D2
Noé [F] 38 B2
Nogaro [F] 30 D4
Nogent [F] 20 E3
Nogent–le–Roi [F] 12 A4
Nogent–le–Rotrou [F] 18 C1
Nogent–sur–Seine [F] 20 B2
Noidans–le–Ferroux [F] 20 F4
Noirétable [F] 26 C4
Noirmoutier–en–l'Ile [F] 16 C3
Nolay [F] 26 F2
Nomeny [F] 22 C1
Nomexy [F] 22 C3
Nonancourt [F] 10 F4

Nonant–le–Pin [F] 10 E4
Nontron [F] 24 D4
Nonza [F] 44 C1
Noordwijk aan Zee [NL] 2 A4
Nordausques [F] 4 B4
Norg [NL] 2 E2
Nort–sur–Erdre [F] 16 D2
Notre–Dame de Consolation [F]
28 D2
Notre–Dame de–la–Roquette
[F] 42 B3
Notre–Dame des Fontaines [F]
42 D2
Nouan–le–Fuzelier [F] 18 E3
Nouans–les–Fontaines [F]
18 C4
Nouvaillé–Maupertuis [F]
24 E2
Nouvion [F] 12 B1
Noves [F] 40 D2
Novion–Porcien [F] 12 F3
Noyant [F] 18 B3
Noyers [F] 20 C3
Noyers–sur–Jabron [F] 40 F1
Noyon [F] 12 D3
Nozay [F] 16 D2
Nozeroy [F] 28 C3
Nueil–les–Aubiers [F] 16 F4
Nuits–St–Georges [F] 28 B2
Nunspeet [NL] 2 C4
Nyons [F] 34 B4

O

O, Château d'– [F] 10 D4
Oberhaslach [F] 22 D2
Ober3i [F] 22 E3
Objat [F] 32 B1
Odoorn [NL] 2 E3
Oëtre, Roche d'– [F] 10 D3
Oiron [F] 18 A4
Oirschot [NL] 6 B3
Oisemont [F] 12 B1
Oissel [F] 12 A3
Oisterwijk [NL] 6 B3
Olargues [F] 38 E2
Oldeberkoop [NL] 2 D3
Oldenzaal [NL] 2 E4
Olen [B] 6 B4
Oletta [F] 44 C2
Olette [F] 38 D4
Olivet [F] 18 E3
Olliergues [F] 32 F1
Olmeto [F] 44 B3
Olonzac [F] 38 E2
Oloron–Ste–Marie [F] 36 D2
Olst [NL] 2 D4
Ommen [NL] 2 D3
Onnaing [F] 12 E1
Ooidonk [B] 4 E4
Oostburg [NL] 4 E3
Oostende [B] 4 D3
Oosterbeek [NL] 6 C2
Oostérénd [NL] 2 C1
Oosterhout [NL] 6 B2
Oosterwolde [NL] 2 D2
Oostmalle [B] 6 A3
Opglabbek [B] 6 C4
Oploo [NL] 6 C3
Oppidum d'Ensérune [F]
38 E2
Oraison [F] 40 F2
Orange [F] 40 D1
Orasi [F] 44 B4
Orbec [F] 10 E3
Orbey [F] 22 D3
Orches [F] 18 B4

Orchies [F] 12 E1
Orcières [F] 34 E4
Orgelet [F] 28 B3
Orgeval [F] 12 B4
Orgnac–l'Aven [F] 34 A4
Orgon [F] 40 D2
Orléans [F] 18 E2
Orly [F] 12 C4
Ornans [F] 28 C2
Orthez [F] 36 D2
Orto [F] 44 B2
Osmoy–St–Valery [F] 12 A1
Oss [NL] 6 C2
Ostwald [F] 22 E2
Ouanne [F] 20 B3
Oucques [F] 18 D2
Oud Beijerland [NL] 6 A2
Ouddorp [NL] 4 F2
Oudenaarde [B] 4 E4
Oude–Pekela [NL] 2 E2
Oudewater [NL] 2 B4
Ouistreham [F] 10 D2
Oullins [F] 34 B1
Ourscamps, Abbaye d'– [F] 12 D3
Oust [F] 38 B3
Ouzouer–le–Marché [F] 18 D2
Overijse [B] 4 F4
Oyonnax [F] 28 B4
Oyrières [F] 22 A4

P

Pacy–sur–Eure [F] 12 A3
Padirac, Gouffre de– [F] 32 B2
Pagnoz [F] 28 C2
Pagny–sur–Moselle [F] 22 C1
Pailhès [F] 38 C2
Paimbo euf [F] 16 D2
Paimpol [F] 8 D2
Paladru [F] 34 D2
Palaiseau [F] 12 B4
Palavas–les–Flots [F] 40 B2
Paliseul [B] 14 B2
Palluau [F] 16 D4
Pamiers [F] 38 C2
Panassac [F] 36 F2
Parata, Tour de la– [F] 44 A3
Paray–le–Monial [F] 26 E3
Parcé sur Sarthe [F] 18 A2
Parentis–en–Born [F] 30 B2
Pargny–sur–Saulx [F] 20 D1
Paris [F] 12 C4
Parisot [F] 32 B3
Parthenay [F] 24 D1
Partinello [F] 44 A2
Pas–en–Artois [F] 12 C1
Patay [F] 18 D2
Pau [F] 36 D2
Pauillac [F] 24 B4
Paulhaguet [F] 32 E2
Paulx [F] 16 D3
Pavilly [F] 10 F2
Payrac [F] 32 B2
Péaule [F] 16 C2
Pech–Merle, Grotte du– [F]
32 B3
Peïra–Cava [F] 42 D2
Pellegrue [F] 30 D2
Pellevoisin [F] 18 C4
Pélussin [F] 34 B2
Pendus, Rocher des– [F] 32 D2
Penestin [F] 16 C2
Penmarch, Pointe de– [F] 8 B4
Pentrez–Plage [F] 8 B3
Percy [F] 10 C3
Père de Montfort, Grotte du– [F]
24 C1

Périers [F] 10 C2
Pérignac [F] 24 C3
Périgueux [F] 30 F1
Perkpolder [NL] 4 E3
Pernes–les–Fontaines [F]
40 D2
Peron [F] 28 C4
Péronne [F] 12 D2
Pérouges [F] 34 C1
Perpignan [F] 38 E4
Perros–Guirec [F] 8 C2
Pertuis [F] 40 E2
Péruwelz [B] 12 E1
Perwez [B] 14 A1
Pesmes [F] 28 C2
Pétange [L] 14 C3
Petreto–Bicchisano [F] 44 B3
Peypin [F] 40 E3
Peyragudes [F] 36 E4
Peyrat–le–Chateaux [F] 26 A4
Peyrehorade [F] 30 B4
Peyriac–Minervois [F] 38 E2
Peyrolles [F] 40 E2
Peyruis [F] 40 F2
Peyrusse–le–Roc [F] 32 C3
Pézenas [F] 38 F2
Pfaffen-Hoffen [F] 22 E2
Phalsbourg [F] 22 D2
Philippeville [F] 14 A2
Piana [F] 44 A2
Pianiccia [F] 44 C2
Pianotolli–Caldarello [F] 44 B4
Picquigny [F] 12 C2
Piedicroce [F] 44 C2
Piennes [F] 14 B4
Pierre–Buffière [F] 24 F4
Pierre–de–Bresse [F] 28 B2
Pierrefitte–Nestalas [F] 36 E3
Pierrefitte–sur–Aire [F] 20 E1
Pierrefonds [F] 12 D3
Pierrefort [F] 32 D2
Pierrefort, Château de– [F]
20 F1
Pierrelatte [F] 34 B4
Pierroton [F] 30 C2
Pietralba [F] 44 B2
Pilat, Dune de– [F] 30 B2
Pilat–Plage [F] 30 B2
Pinarellu [F] 44 B4
Piney [F] 20 C2
Pino [F] 44 C1
Pinols [F] 32 D2
Pionsat [F] 26 C3
Pipriac [F] 16 D1
Piriac–sur–Mer [F] 16 C2
Pirou–Plage [F] 10 B2
Pissos [F] 30 C3
Pithiviers [F] 18 E2
Plabennec [F] 8 B2
Plage de Pineto [F] 44 C2
Plaigne [F] 38 C2
Plaisance [F] 36 E2
Plancoët [F] 8 E3
Plan d' Orgon [F] 40 D2
Plan–du–Lac [F] 34 F1
Pleaux [F] 32 C2
Plélan–le–Grand [F] 16 D1
Plémet [F] 8 D4
Plesse [F] 16 D2
Plessis–Bourré, Château du– [F]
16 F2
Plestin–les–Grèves [F] 8 C2
Pleumartin [F] 24 E1
Pleyben [F] 8 B3
Ploërmel [F] 16 D1
Plombières–les–Bains [F]
22 C3
Plonéour Lanvern [F] 8 B4
Plouaret [F] 8 C3
Plouay [F] 8 C4
Ploubalay [F] 8 E3
Ploudalmézeau [F] 8 B2

Plouescat [F] 8 B2
Plougasnou [F] 8 C2
Plougastel–Daoulas [F] 8 B3
Plougonven [F] 8 C3
Plouguenast [F] 8 D4
Plouguerneau [F] 8 B2
Plouha [F] 8 D3
Plouigneau [F] 8 C3
Ploumanac'h [F] 8 C2
Plounévez–Quintin [F] 8 C3
Plouray [F] 8 C4
Plozévet [F] 8 B4
Pluviers [F] 24 E4
Pluvigner [F] 16 B1
Podensac [F] 30 D2
Poeldijk [NL] 2 A4
Pointe des Poulains [F] 16 B2
Point Sublime [F] 32 D4
Poissons [F] 20 E2
Poitiers [F] 24 E2
Poix [F] 12 B2
Poligny [F] 28 C2
Pompey [F] 22 C2
Poncin [F] 28 B4
Podensac [F] 30 D2
Pons [F] 24 C3
Pont [F] 28 B2
Pontacq [F] 36 E3
Pontailler–sur–Saône [F]
28 B1
Pont–à–Mousson [F]
22 C1
Pontarion [F] 26 A3
Pontarlier [F] 28 D2
Pontaubault [F] 10 B3
Pont–Audemer [F] 10 E2
Pontaumur [F] 26 C4
Pont–Aven [F] 8 B4
Pont Cellier [F] 26 C3
Pontcharra [F] 34 D2
Pontchartrain [F] 12 B4
Pontchâteau [F] 16 D2
Pont–Croix [F] 8 A3
Pont–d'Ain [F] 28 B4
Pont–de–Briques [F] 4 B4
Pont–de–Dore [F] 26 D4
Pont–de–l'Arche [F] 12 A3
Pont–de–Roide [F] 28 D2
Pont–de–Salars [F] 32 D4
Pont–d'Espagne [F] 36 D3
Pont–de–Vaux [F] 28 A3
Ponte–Leccia [F] 44 B2
Pont–en–Royans [F] 34 C3
Ponte Nuovo [F] 44 C2
Pontenx–les–Forges [F]
30 B2–3
Pontgibaud [F] 26 C4
Pontigny [F] 20 B3
Pontivy [F] 8 D4
Pont–l'Abbé [F] 8 B4
Pont–l'Evêque [F] 10 E2
Pontlevoy [F] 18 C3
Pontoise [F] 12 B3
Pontorson [F] 8 F3
Pontpierre [L] 14 C3
Pont–Réan [F] 16 D1
Pontrieux [F] 8 D3
Pont–Scorff [F] 8 C4
Pont–St–Esprit [F] 40 D1
Pont–St–Vincent [F]
22 C2
Pont–sur–Yonne [F] 20 B2
Pontvallain [F] 18 B2
Poperinge [B] 4 C4
Pornic [F] 16 C3
Pornichet [F] 16 C2
Porquerolles [F] 40 F4
Portbail [F] 10 B2
Port–Barcarès [F] 38 E3
Port–Camargue [F] 40 C2
Port–Cros [F] 42 B4
Port–de–Bouc [F] 40 D3

Port-en-Bessin [F] 10 D2
Portes les Valence [F] 34 B3
Port-Grimaud [F] 42 B3
Porticcio [F] 44 B3
Port-Joinville [F] 16 C4
Port-la-Nouvelle [F] 38 E3
Port-Leucate [F] 38 E3
Port-Louis [F] 16 B1
Port-Manech [F] 8 B4
Port-Navalo [F] 16 B2
Porto [F] 44 A2
Porto-Pollo [F] 44 B3
Porto-Vecchio [F] 44 B4
Port-Ste-Marie [F] 30 E3
Port-St-Louis-du-Rhône [F]
    40 D3
Port-St-Marie, la Chartreuse
    de- [F] 26 C4
Port-sur-Saône [F] 20 F4
Port-Vendres [F] 38 E4
Pouancé [F] 16 E2
Pougues-les-Eaux [F] 26 D1
Pouilly [F] 18 F4
Pouilly-en-Auxois [F] 26 F1
Pouilly-sous-Charlieu [F]
    26 E4
Poussay [F] 22 B3
Pouyastruc [F] 36 E3
Pouy-de-Touges [F] 38 B2
Pouzauges [F] 16 E4
Pouzihac [F] 40 D1
Pradelle [F] 34 C4
Pradelles [F] 32 F3
Prades [F] 38 D4
Prahecq [F] 24 C2
Pralognan-la-Vanoise [F]
    34 E2
Prats-de-Mollo-la-Preste [F]
    38 D4
Prauthoy [F] 20 E4
Préchac [F] 30 C3
Précy-sous-Thil [F]
    20 C4
Precy Sur Vrin [F] 20 B3
Pré-en-Pail [F] 10 D4
Prémery [F] 26 D1
Prénouvellon [F] 18 D2
Pressac [F] 24 E3
Preuilly-sur-Claise [F]
    24 F1
Préveranges [F] 26 B2
Primel-Trégastel [F] 8 C2
Prissac [F] 24 F2
Profondeville [B] 14 A1
Propriano [F] 44 B3
Prouille [F] 38 D2
Provins [F] 20 B1
Prunet [F] 32 C3
Prunete [F] 44 C2
Prunet-et-Belpuig [F]
    38 D4
Puget-sur-Argens [F]
    42 B3
Puget-Théniers [F] 42 C2
Puget-Ville [F] 40 F3
Puiseaux [F] 18 F2
Puivert [F] 38 D3
Punta, château de la– [F]
    44 A3
Purmerend [NL] 2 B3
Putanges-Pont-Ecrepin [F]
    10 D3
Puttelange [F] 22 D1
Putten [NL] 2 C4
Puyvaladar [F] 38 D3
Puyguilhem [F] 24 E4
Puy-Guillaume [F] 26 D4
Puylaurens [F] 38 D2
Puy-l'Evêque [F] 30 F3
Puymorens, Col de– [F]
    38 C4
Pyla-sur-Mer [F] 30 B2

Q

Qiselay-et-Graciaux [F] 28 C1
Quarré-les-Tombes [F] 20 C4
Qudeschild [NL] 2 B2
Quelaines–St. Gault [F] 16 F2
Quercamps [F] 4 B4
Quéribus, Château de– [F]
    38 D3
Quéroy, Grottes du– [F] 24 D4
Questembert [F] 16 C2
Quettehou [F] 10 C1
Quiberon [F] 16 B2
Quillan [F] 38 D3
Quimper [F] 8 B4
Quimperlé [F] 8 C4
Quinéville [F] 10 C1
Quingey [F] 28 C2
Quintin [F] 8 D3
Quissac [F] 40 C2

R

Raalte [NL] 2 D4
Rabastens [F] 38 C1
Rabastens-de-Bigorre [F]
    36 E2
Raival [F] 20 E1
Rambervillers [F] 22 C3
Rambouillet [F] 18 E1
Randan [F] 26 D4
Rânes [F] 10 D4
Raon-l'Etape [F] 22 D3
Raulach [F] 32 D2
Ravel [F] 26 D4
Rayol [F] 42 B4
Réalmont [F] 38 D1
Réau, Ancient Abbaye de la– [F]
    24 E2
Réaup-Lisse [F] 30 D3
Rebais [F] 12 D4
Recey-sur-Ource [F] 20 D3
Recologne [F] 28 C2
Redon [F] 16 D2
Reichstett [F] 22 E2
Reignier [F] 28 C4
Reillanne [F] 40 E2
Reims [F] 12 E4
Rely [F] 4 C4
Rémalard [F] 18 C1
Remich [L] 14 C3
Remiremont [F] 22 C3
Remouchamps [B] 14 C1
Remoulins [F] 40 D2
Rémuzat [F] 34 C4
Renaison [F] 26 E4
Renaix (Ronse) [B] 4 E4
Renkum [NL] 6 C2
Rennes [F] 16 E1
République, Col de la– [F]
    34 B2
Réquista [F] 32 C4
Ressons [F] 12 C3
Rethel [F] 14 A4
Retie [B] 6 B3
Retiers [F] 16 E1
Retournac [F] 32 F2
Reuilly [F] 18 E4
Reusel [NL] 6 B3
Revel [F] 38 D2
Révigny-sur-Ornain [F] 20 E1
Revin [F] 14 A2
Rhenen [NL] 6 C2

Rhinau [F] 22 E3
Rhoon [NL] 6 A2
Riaillé [F] 16 E2
Rians [F] 40 E3
Ribeauville [F] 22 D3
Ribécourt [F] 12 D3
Ribemont [F] 12 E2
Richelieu [F] 18 B4
Ridderkerk [NL] 6 B2
Rieumes [F] 38 B2
Rieupeyroux [F] 32 C3
Rieussec [F] 38 E2
Rieux [F] 38 B2
Riez [F] 40 F2
Rignac [F] 32 C3
Rijssen [NL] 2 D4
Rillé [F] 18 B3
Rimaucourt [F] 20 E3
Riom [F] 26 C4
Riom-ès-Montagnes [F]
    32 D2
Rion-des-Landes [F] 30 B3
Rioz [F] 28 C1
Riquewihr [F] 22 D3
Riscle [F] 30 C4
Riva-Bella [F] 10 D2
Rive-de-Gier [F] 34 B2
Rivesaltes [F] 38 E3
Roanne [F] 26 E4
Robertingue [F] 4 B4
Rocamadour [F] 32 B2
Rochebloine, Château de– [F]
    34 B3
Rochechouart [F] 24 E3
Rochecourbière, Grotte de– [F]
    34 B4
Rochefort [B] 14 B2
Rochefort [F] 24 B2
Rochefort, Grotte de– [F]
    18 A2
Rochefort-en-Terre [F] 16 C1
Rochefort-s-Nenon [F] 28 B2
Rochehaut [B] 14 A3
Rochemaure [F] 34 B4
Rocher, Château du– [F] 18 A1
Rocherolle, Château de la– [F]
    26 A2
Rochers, Château des– [F]
    16 E1
Rocheservière [F] 16 D3
Rocroi [F] 12 F2
Rodange [L] 14 B3
Roden [NL] 2 D2
Rodez [F] 32 C3
Roermond [NL] 6 C4
Roeselare (Roulers) [B] 4 D4
Roeulx [F] 12 F1
Rogliano [F] 44 C1
Rognac [F] 40 D3
Rohan [F] 8 D4
Rohrbach-lès-Bitche [F]
    22 D1
Roisel [F] 12 D2
Romans-sur-Isère [F] 34 C3
Rombas [F] 14 C4
Romilly-sur-Seine [F] 20 C2
Romorantin-Lanthenay [F]
    18 D4
Ronchamp [F] 22 C4
Ronse (Renaix) [B] 4 E4
Roodeschool [NL] 2 E2
Roosendaal [NL] 4 F4
Roque, Pointe de la– [F] 10 E2
Roquebillière [F] 42 D2
Roquebrune-Cap-Martin [F]
    42 D3
Roquefort [F] 30 C3
Roquefort-sur-Soulzon [F]
    38 F1
Roquemaure [F] 40 D1
Roqueteson [F] 42 C2

Roquetaillade, Château de– [F]
    30 D2
Rosans [F] 34 C4
Roscoff [F] 8 C2
Rosny Sur Seine [F] 12 B3
Rosporden [F] 8 B4
Rostassac [F] 30 F3
Rostrenen [F] 8 C3
Rothéneuf [F] 8 F3
Rotterdam [NL] 6 A2
Roubaix [F] 4 E4
Rouen [F] 12 A2
Rouffach [F] 22 D4
Rouffignac, Grotte de– [F]
    30 F2
Rougé [F] 16 E2
Rougemont [F] 22 D4
Rougemont [F] 28 D1
Rouillac [F] 24 C3
Roujan [F] 38 F2
Roulers (Roeselare) [B] 4 D4
Roussillon [F] 40 E2
Roussillon [F] 34 B2
Rouvres-en-Xaintois [F] 20 F3
Royan [F] 24 B3
Royat [F] 26 C4
Royaumont, Abbaye de– [F]
    12 C3
Roybon [F] 34 C2
Roye [F] 12 D2
Royère-de-Vassivière [F]
    26 A4
Rozay-en-Brie [F] 20 B1
Rozoy [F] 12 E3
Rue [F] 12 B1
Ruelle-sur-Touvre [F] 24 D3
Ruffec [F] 24 D3
Ruffieux [F] 34 D1
Rugles [F] 10 E4
Rumigny [F] 12 F2
Rumilly [F] 34 D1
Rummen [B] 6 B4
Rumont [F] 20 E2
Rupt [F] 22 C4
Ruurlo [NL] 6 D2

S

Saales [F] 22 D3
Sables-d'Or-les-Pins [F] 8 E3
Sablé-sur-Sarthe [F] 18 A2
Sabres [F] 30 C3
Saeul [L] 14 C3
Sagone [F] 44 A3
Saillagouse [F] 38 C4
Sailly Flibeaucourt [F] 12 B1
Sains [F] 12 E2
Saint Albain [F] 28 A3
Sainte-Lucie-de-Tallano [F] 44
    B3
Sainte-Marie-Siché [F] 44 B3
Saintes [F] 24 C3
Saint-Ghislain [B] 12 E1
Saint Hilaire de la Côte [F] 34
    C2
Saissac [F] 38 D2
Salau [F] 38 B3
Salbris [F] 18 E3
Salernes [F] 40 F3
Salers [F] 32 D2
Salice [F] 44 B3
Salies-de-Béarn [F] 30 B4
Salies-du-Salat [F] 38 B2
Salignac-Eyvigues [F] 32 B2
Salin-de-Giraud [F] 40 D3
Salins-les-Bains [F] 28 C2
Sallanches [F] 34 E1

Salles [F] 30 C2
Salles-Curan [F] 32 D4
Salles-s.-l'Hers [F] 38 C2
Salon [F] 20 C2
Salon-de-Provence [F] 40 D2
Salses-le-Château [F] 38 E3
Salvagnac [F] 32 B4
Salviac [F] 30 F2
Samadet [F] 30 C4
Samadet [F] 30 C4
Samatan [F] 38 B1
Samer [F] 4 B4
Samoëns [F] 34 F1
Sanary-sur-Mer [F] 40 E4
Sancergues [F] 26 D1
Sancerre [F] 18 F4
Sancey-le-Grand [F] 28 D2
Sauclières [F] 38 F1
Sancoins [F] 26 C2
Sancy-sur-Nied [F] 22 C1
Sandaucourt [F] 20 F3
Sanguinet [F] 30 B2
Santa Severa [F] 44 C1
Sanxay [F] 24 D2
Sanzay [F] 16 F4
Saorge [F] 42 D2
Saou [F] 34 B4
Sappemeer [NL] 2 E2
Saramon [F] 38 B1
Sari d'Orcino [F] 44 B3
Sarlat-la-Canéda [F] 32 A2
Sarralbe [F] 22 D1
Sarrebourg [F] 22 D2
Sarreguemines [F] 22 D1
Sarron [F] 30 C4
Sartène [F] 44 B4
Sartilly [F] 10 B3
Sarzeau [F] 16 C2
Sassenage [F] 34 D3
Sassenheim [NL] 2 B4
Saucats [F] 30 C2
Saudron [F] 20 E2
Saugues [F] 32 E2
Saujon [F] 24 B3
Saulieu [F] 26 F1
Sault [F] 40 E1
Sault-de-Navailles [F] 36 D2
Saulvaux [F] 22 B2
Saulx [F] 22 B4
Saulxures [F] 22 C4
Saumur [F] 18 A3
Sausheim [F] 22 D4
Sauvagnat [F] 26 B4
Sauve [F] 40 C1
Sauveterre-de-Béarn [F]
    36 C2
Sauveterre-de-Guyenne [F]
    30 D2
Sauviant-sur-Vige [F] 24 F3
Sauxillanges [F] 32 E1
Sauzet [F] 30 F3
Sauzé-Vaussais [F] 24 D2
Sauzon [F] 16 B2
Savenay [F] 16 D2
Saverdun [F] 38 C2
Saverne [F] 22 D2
Savignac-les-Eglises [F]
    30 F1
Savigny-sur-Braye [F] 18 C2
Savines-le-Lac [F] 34 E4
Scaër [F] 8 C4
Schagen [NL] 2 B3
Scheveningen [NL] 2 A4
Schiermonnikoog [NL] 2 D1
Schilde [B] 6 A3
Schirmeck [F] 22 D3
Schlosspark [F] 22 E2
Schoondijke [NL] 4 E3
Schoonebeek [NL] 2 E3
Schoonhoven [NL] 6 B2
Schoonoord [NL] 2 E3

Scrignac [F] 8 C3
Secondigny [F] 24 C1
Sedan [F] 14 A3
Séderon [F] 40 E1
Sées [F] 10 E4
Segonzac [F] 24 C3
Segré [F] 16 F2
Seiches-sur-le-Loir [F] 18 A2
Seilhac [F] 32 B1
Seilleraye, Château de la– [F] 16 D3
Seissan [F] 36 F2
Sélestat [F] 22 D3
Selles [F] 18 D4
Sellières [F] 28 B2
Selongey [F] 20 E4
Selonnet [F] 42 B1
Seltz [F] 22 F2
Semur-en-Auxois [F] 20 C4
Sénas [F] 40 D2
Seneffe [B] 12 F1
Senez [F] 42 B2
Senlis [F] 12 C3
Sennecey-le-Grand [F] 28 A3
Senonches [F] 10 F4
Senones [F] 22 D3
Sens [F] 20 B2
Sens-de-Bretagne [F] 8 F4
Senseruth [B] 14 A3
Sept-Saulx [F] 12 E4
Serain [F] 12 E2
Seraincourt [F] 12 F3
Seraing [B] 14 B1
Sérent [F] 16 C1
Sermaize-les-Bains [F] 20 E1
Serrant, Château de– [F] 16 F3
Serres [F] 34 C4
Serrières [F] 34 B2
Servian [F] 38 F2
Sète [F] 40 B3
Seurre [F] 28 B2
Sévérac-le-Château [F] 32 D4
Sevrier [F] 34 E1
Seyches [F] 30 E2
Seyne [F] 42 B1
Seynod [F] 34 D1
Seyssel [F] 34 D1
Seysses [F] 38 C1
Sézanne [F] 20 C1
's Heerenberg [NL] 6 D2
's-Hertogenbosch [NL] 6 B2
Siddeburen [NL] 2 E2
Siecq [F] 24 C3
Sierck-les-Bains [F] 14 C4
Sierentz [F] 28 F1
Sigean [F] 38 E3
Signes [F] 40 E3
Signy-l'Abbaye [F] 12 F3
Sillans-la-Cascade [F] 40 F3
Sillé-le-Guillaume [F] 18 B1
Silvacane [F] 40 E2
Simorre [F] 36 F2
Sion [F] 22 B2
Siorac-en-Périgord [F] 30 F2
Sissonne [F] 12 E3
Sisteron [F] 40 F1
Sittard [NL] 6 C4
Sivry-sur-Meuse [F] 14 B4
Six-Fours-les-Plages [F] 40 E4
Sixt-Fer-à Cheval [F] 34 F1
Sizun [F] 8 B3
Sliedrecht [NL] 6 B2
Sloten [NL] 2 C3
Sluis [NL] 4 E3
Sluis [NL] 4 F2
Smilde [NL] 2 D3
Sneek [NL] 2 C2
Sochaux [F] 28 E1
Soest [NL] 2 C4
Soestdijk [NL] 2 C4

Soignies [B] 12 F1
Soissons [F] 12 D3
Solenzara [F] 44 C3
Solesmes [F] 12 E2
Solesmes, Abbaye de– [F] 18 A2
Solignac [F] 24 F4
Solliès-Pont [F] 40 F4
Solutré, Roche de– [F] 26 F3
Sombernon [F] 28 A1
Someren [NL] 6 C3
Sommepy-Tahure [F] 12 F4
Sommery [F] 12 AB2
Sommesous [F] 20 C1
Sommières [F] 40 C2
Sompuis [F] 20 D1
Sore [F] 30 C3
Sorgues [F] 40 D2
Sospel [F] 42 D2
Sotta [F] 44 B4
Sotteville Les Rouen [F] 12 A2
Soual [F] 38 D2
Souesmes [F] 18 E3
Soufflenheim [F] 22 E2
Souillac [F] 32 B2
Souilly [F] 20 E1
Soulac-sur-Mere [F] 24 B3
Soulaines-Dhuys [F] 20 D2
Soultz [F] 22 D4
Soultz [F] 22 E2
Soumoulou [F] 36 E3
Souppes-sur-Loing [F] 18 F2
Sourdeval [F] 10 C3
Sourdon [F] 12 C2
Sournia [F] 38 D3
Sousceyrac [F] 32 C2
Soustons [F] 30 B3
Souvigny [F] 26 D3
Spa [B] 14 C1
Spakenburg [NL] 2 C4
Spijkenisse [NL] 4 F2
Spincourt [F] 14 B4
Spy [B] 14 A1
Stadskanaal [NL] 2 E3
St-Affrique [F] 38 E1
St-Agnant [F] 24 B3
St-Agrève [F] 34 B3
St-Aignan [F] 16 E2
St-Aignan [F] 18 D4
Stainville [F] 20 E2
St-Alban [F] 32 E3
St-Amand-en-Puisaye [F] 20 A4
St-Amand-les-Eaux [F] 12 E1
St-Amand-Longpré [F] 18 C3
St-Amand-Montrond [F] 26 C2
St-Amans [F] 32 E3
St-Amant-Roche-Savine [F] 32 F1
St-Ambroix [F] 32 F4
St-Amé [F] 22 C3
St-Amour [F] 28 B3
St-André [F] 12 A4
St-André-de-Cubzac [F] 30 D1
St-André-les-Alpes [F] 42 B2
St Annaparochie [NL] 2 D2
St-Anthème [F] 32 F1
St-Antoine [F] 34 C2
St.-Antoine, Chapelle– [F] 36 C2
St-Antonin-Noble-Val [F] 32 B4
St.Antonino [F] 44 B2
St-Août [F] 26 B2
Staphorst [NL] 2 D3
St-Astier [F] 30 E1
St-Aubane [F] 42 C2
St-Auban-sur-l'Ouvèze [F] 40 E1
St-Aubin-d'Aubigné [F] 8 F4

St-Aubin-du-Cormier [F] 8 F4
St-Aubin-sur-Mer [F] 10 D2
St.-Augustin, Château de– [F] 26 C2
St-Aulaye [F] 30 E1
Stavelot [B] 14 C2
Stavenisse [NL] 4 F2
Staveren [NL] 2 C3
St-Avold [F] 22 D1
St-Ayguif [F] 42 B3
St-Bard [F] 26 B4
St.-Barthélemy [F] 10 C3
St-Béat [F] 36 F4
St-Beauzély [F] 32 D4
St-Benin [F] 26 D2
St-Benoît-du-Sault [F] 24 F2
St-Benoît-sur-Loire [F] 18 E3
St-Bertrand-de-Comminges [F] 36 F3
St.-Blaise [F] 40 D3
St-Blin [F] 20 E3
St-Bonnet-de-Joux [F] 26 F3
St-Bonnet-en-Champsaur [F] 34 D4
St-Bonnet-le-Château [F] 32 F2
St-Brevin-les-Pins [F] 16 C3
St-Brice-en-Coglès [F] 10 B4
St-Brieuc [F] 8 D3
St-Calais [F] 18 C2
St-Cast-le-Guildo [F] 8 E3
St-Céré [F] 32 B2
St-Cernin [F] 32 C2
St-Chamas [F] 40 D3
St-Chamond [F] 34 B2
St-Chély-d'Apcher [F] 32 E3
St-Chély-d'Aubrac [F] 32 D3
St-Chinian [F] 38 E2
St.Christophe-en-Oisans [F] 34 D3
St-Ciers-sur-Gironde [F] 24 B4
St-Cirq-Lapopie [F] 32 B3
St.-Clair [F] 10 D2
St-Clar [F] 30 E4
St-Claud [F] 24 D3
St-Claude [F] 28 C3
St-Clément [F] 22 C2
St-Clément-sur-Durance [F] 34 E4
St-Côme-d'Olt [F] 32 D3
St.-Cosme-en-Vairais [F] 18 C1
St-Cyprien [F] 30 F2
St-Cyprien-Plage [F] 38 E4
St-Denis [F] 12 C4
St-Denis d'Oléron [F] 24 B2
St-Denis d'Orques [F] 18 A2
St-Didier-en-Velay [F] 34 A2
St-Dié [F] 22 D3
St-Dizier [F] 20 E2
St-Donat-sur-l'Herbasse [F] 34 B3
Ste-Anne-d'Auray [F] 16 B1
Ste-Anne-la-Palud [F] 8 B3
Ste.-Barbe [F] 8 A4
Ste-Croix-Volvestre [F] 38 B2
Steenbergen [NL] 4 F3
Ste.-Engrâce [F] 36 C3
Ste-Enimie [F] 32 E4
Steenvoorde [F] 4 C4
Steenwijk [NL] 2 D3
Ste-Foy-la-Grande [F] 30 E2
Ste-Gauburge-Ste-Colombe [F] 10 E4
St-Egrève [F] 34 D2
Ste-Hélène [F] 30 C1
Ste-Hermine [F] 24 B1
Ste.- Jalle [F] 40 E1
Ste-Livrade-sur-Lot [F] 30 E3
Stellendam [NL] 4 F2
St-Eloy-les-Mines [F] 26 C3

Ste-Marie-aux-Mines [F] 22 D3
Ste-Marie-de-Campan [F] 36 E3
Ste-Maure-de-Touraine [F] 18 B4
Ste-Maxime [F] 42 B3
Ste-Menehould [F] 14 A4
Ste-Mère-du-Mont [F] 10 C2
Ste-Mère-Eglise [F] 10 C2
St-Emilion [F] 30 D2
Stenay [F] 14 B3
Ste-Sévère [F] 26 B2
Stes-Maries-de-la-Mer [F] 40 C3
St. Estèphe [F] 24 B4
Ste-Suzanne [F] 18 A1
St-Étienne [F] 34 B2
St-Étienne [F] 40 F2
St-Étienne-de-Baïgorry [F] 36 C2
St-Étienne-de-St-Geoirs [F] 34 C2
St-Étienne-de-Tinée [F] 42 C2
Ste-Tulle [F] 40 E2
St-Fargeau [F] 20 A3
St-Fiacre [F] 30 D2
St-Firmin [F] 34 D3
St-Florent [F] 16 E3
St-Florent [F] 26 B1
St-Florent [F] 44 C1
St.-Florent-des-Bois [F] 16 D4
St-Florentin [F] 20 B3
St-Flour [F] 32 E2
St-Fort-sur-Gironde [F] 24 B4
St.-Fort-sur-le-Né [F] 24 C3
St-Fulgent [F] 16 E4
St-Galmier [F] 34 B1
St-Gaudens [F] 36 F3
St-Gaultier [F] 26 A2
St-Geniez-d'Olt [F] 32 D3
St-Genis-de-Saintonge [F] 24 C4
St-Genix-sur-Guiers [F] 34 D2
St-Georges [F] 16 F3
St-Georges-de-Didonne [F] 24 B3
St. Georges-on-Couzan [F] 32 F1
St-Geours-de-Maremne [F] 30 B4
St-Germain [F] 12 B4
St-Germain [F] 24 F4
St-Germain-de-Calberte [F] 32 E4
St-Germain-de-Joux [F] 28 B4
St-Germain-des-Fossés [F] 26 D3
St-Germain-des-Vaux [F] 10 B1
St-Germain-du-Bois [F] 28 B3
St-Germain-du-Plain [F] 28 A3
St-Germain-Laval [F] 26 E4
St-Germain-Lembron [F] 32 E1
St-Germain-l'Herm [F] 32 E1
St-Germain-Plage [F] 10 B2
St-Germer-de-Fly [F] 12 B3
St-Gervais [F] 38 E2
St-Gervais-d'Auvergne [F] 26 C3
St-Gervais-les-Bains [F] 34 E1
St-Gildas-des-Bois [F] 16 D2
St-Gilles [F] 40 C2
St-Gilles-Croix-de-Vie [F] 16 C4

St-Gilles-Pligeaux [F] 8 D3
St-Girons [F] 38 B2
St-Girons-en-Marensin [F] 30 B3
St-Girons-Plage [F] 30 B3
St-Gobain [F] 12 D3
St-Gorgon-Main [F] 28 D2
St-Guénolé [F] 8 A4
St-Guilhem-le-Desert [F] 40 B2
St. Hilaire Cottes [F] 4 C4
St-Hilaire-de-Villefranche [F] 24 C3
St-Hilaire-du-Harcouët [F] 10 C3
St-Hippolyte [F] 28 D2
St-Hippolyte-du-Fort [F] 40 B1
St-Honoré les-Bains [F] 26 E2
St-Hubert [B] 14 B2
Stiens [NL] 2 D2
St-Jacut [F] 8 E3
St-James [F] 10 B3
St-Jean-Brévelay [F] 16 C1
St-Jean-Cap-Ferrat [F] 42 C3
St-Jean-d'Angély [F] 24 C3
St-Jean-de-Bournay [F] 34 C2
St-Jean-de-Losne [F] 28 B2
St-Jean-de-Luz [F] 36 B2
St-Jean-de-Maurienne [F] 34 E3
St-Jean-de-Monts [F] 16 C3
St-Jean-du-Bruel [F] 38 F1
St-Jean-du-Gard [F] 40 C1
St-Jean-du-Liget, Chapelle– [F] 18 C4
St-Jean-en-Royans [F] 34 C3
St-Jean-le-Thomas [F] 10 B3
St-Jean-Pied-de-Port [F] 36 C2
St. Jeans-d'Arves [F] 34 E3
St-Jeoire [F] 28 D4
St.-Jores [F] 10 C2
St-Jorioz [F] 34 E1
St-Jory [F] 38 C1
St-Jouan-de-l'Isle [F] 8 E4
St-Jouin-de-Marnes [F] 18 A4
St-Juéry [F] 38 D1
St-Julien [F] 28 B3
St-Julien [F] 38 B2
St-Julien-Chapteuil [F] 32 F2
St-Julien-de-Vouvantes [F] 16 E2
St. Julien-du-Verdon [F] 42 B2
St-Julien-en-Beauchène [F] 34 C4
St-Julien-en-Born [F] 30 B3
St-Julien-en-Genevois [F] 28 C4
St-Julien-l'Ars [F] 24 E2
St-Junien [F] 24 E3
St-Just-en-Chaussée [F] 12 C3
St-Just-en-Chevalet [F] 26 D4
St-Justin [F] 30 C3
St-Lary-Soulan [F] 36 E4
St-Laurent [F] 10 C2
St-Laurent [F] 24 E3
St-Laurent-des-Autels [F] 16E3
St.-Laurent-de-la-Cabrerisse [F] 38 E3
St.-Laurent-de-la-Salanque [F] 38 E4
St.-Laurent-en-Gâtines [F] 18 C3
St-Laurent-en-Grandvaux [F] 28 C3
St-Laurent-les-Bains [F] 32 F3

St-Laurent-Médoc [F] 24 B4
St-Leger [F] 26 E2
St.-Léon, Chapelle- [F] 22 D2
St-Léonard-de-Noblat [F] 24 F3
St-Leu-d'Esserent [F] 12 C3
St-Lizier [F] 38 B2
St-Lô [F] 10 C2
St-Louis [F] 28 F1
St-Loup-sur-Semouse [F]
　22 C4
St-Lunaire [F] 8 E3
St-Lys [F] 38 B1
St-Macaire [F] 30 D2
St-Maclou [F] 10 E2
St-Maixent-l'Ecole [F] 24 D2
St-Malo [F] 8 E3
St-Mamest [F] 30 E2
St-Marcel [F] 34 E2
St-Marcellin [F] 34 C3
St. Marcellin-en-Forez [F]
　34 A2
St-Mars-la-Jaille [F] 16 E2
St. Martin [F] 16 C1
St-Martin-d'Auxigny [F] 18 E4
St-Martin-de-Londres [F]
　40 B2
St. Martin-d'Entraunes [F]
　42 C2
St-Martin-de-Ré [F] 24 B2
St.-Martin-du-Canigou [F]
　38 D4
St-Martin-Lestra [F] 34 B1
St-Martin-l'Heureux [F] 12 F4
St-Martin-Vésubie [F] 42 C2
St-Martory [F] 38 B2
St-Mathieu [F] 24 E4
St.-Mathieu, Pointe de- [F]
　8 A3
St-Mathieu-de-Tréviers [F]
　40 B2
St-Maurice-la-Clouère [F]
　24 E2
St.Maurice la Sotterraine [F]
　24 F3
St.-Maurice-Navacelles [F]
　40 B2
St Maurice-sur-Moselle [F]
　22 C4
St-Maximin-la-Ste-Baume [F]
　40 F3
St-Méen [F] 8 E4
St.-Michel-de Cuxa [F] 38 D4
St-Michel-de-Maurienne [F]
　34 E3
St.Michel de Rieufret [F] 30 C2
St-Michel-en-Grève [F] 8 C2
St-Michel-en-l'Herm [F]
　24 B2
St-Michel-Mont-Mercure [F]
　16 E4
St-Mihiel [F] 20 F1
St-Morand [F] 28 E1
St-Nazaire [F] 16 D2
St.Nazaire Les Eymes [F] 34 D2
St-Nectaire [F] 32 E1
St.-Nicodème [F] 8 D4
St-Nicolas [F] 16 D2
St Nicolas-de-Port [F] 22 C2
St-Nicolas-du-Pélem [F] 8 D3
St-Niklaas [B] 4 F3
St Oedenrode [NL] 6 C3
St-Omer [F] 4 C4
St.-Oswald [F] 14 C4
St-Ouen [F] 12 C1
St-Palais [F] 36 D2
St-Palais-sur-Mer [F] 24 B3
St-Pardoux-la-Rivière [F]
　24 E4
St-Paul [F] 42 C3
St-Paul [F] 42 C1
St-Paul-Cap-de-Joux [F]
　38 D1

St-Paul-de-Fenouillet [F]
　38 D3
St-Pauliene [F] 32 F2
St-Paul-lès-Dax [F] 30 B4
St-Pé [F] 36 D3
St-Péray [F] 34 B3
St-Père [F] 20 B4
St-Père-en-Retz [F] 16 C3
St-Péver [F] 8 D3
St-Philbert [F] 16 D3
St-Pierre-d'Albigny [F] 34 E2
St-Pierre-de-Chartreuse [F]
　34 D2
St-Pierre-de-Chignac [F]
　30 F1
St-Pierre d'Extravache [F]
　34 E3
St-Pierre-d'Oléron [F] 24 B2
St-Pierre-Église [F] 10 C1
St-Pierre-en-Port [F] 10 EF1
St-Pierre-le-Moûtier [F]
　26 D2
St-Pierre-Quiberon [F] 16 B2
St-Pierre-sur-Dives [F] 10 D3
St-Pois [F] 10 C3
St-Pol-de-Léon [F] 8 C2
St-Pons-de-Thomieres [F]
　38 E2
St-Porchaire [F] 24 B3
St-Pourçain sur-Sioule [F]
　26 D3
St.Priest [F] 34 C1
St-Privat [F] 32 C2
St-Quay-Portrieux [F] 8 D3
St.-Quen-en-Belin [F] 18 B2
St-Quentin [F] 12 D2
St-Rambert [F] 34 A2
St-Rambert-d'Albon [F] 34 B2
St-Rambert-en-Bugey [F]
　34 C1
St-Raphaël [F] 42 B3
Strasbourg [F] 22 E2
St-Rémy-de-Provence [F]
　40 D2
St-Renan [F] 8 B3
St.-Révérien [F] 26 D1
St-Riquier [F] 12 C1
St.-Roman, Abbaye de- [F]
　40 D2
St-Rome-de-Tarn [F] 38 E1
St.-Sabin, Chapelle- [F] 30 D3
St-Saëns [F] 12 A2
St.-Samson-la-Poterie [F]
　12 B2
St-Satur [F] 18 F4
St-Saturnin-lès-Apt [F] 40 E2
St-Saulge [F] 26 D1
St-Sauvant [F] 24 D2
St-Sauveur-en-Puisaye [F]
　20 B3
St-Sauveur-le-Vicomte [F]
　10 B2
St-Sauveur-sur-Tinée [F]
　42 C2
St-Savin [F] 30 D1
St-Savin-sur-Gartempe [F]
　24 E2
St-Seine-l'Abbaye [F] 20 D4
St-Sernin-sur-Rance [F]
　38 E1
St-Sever [F] 10 C3
St-Sever [F] 30 C4
St-Sulpice [F] 38 C1
St. Sulpice-Les-Feuilles [F]
　24 F2
St-Symphorien [F] 30 C2
St-Symphorien-de-Lay [F]
　26 E4
St-Symphorien-d'Ozon [F]
　34 C1
St-Symphorien-sur-Coise [F]
　34 B1

St-Thégonnec [F] 8 C3
St-Thiébault [F] 20 E3
St-Trivier-de-Courtes [F]
　28 B3
St-Tropez [F] 42 B3
St.-Ulrich, Château- [F] 22 D3
St-Vaast-la-Hougue [F] 10 C1
St-Valery-en-Caux [F] 10 F1
St-Valery-sur-Somme [F]
　12 B1
St-Vallier-de-Thiey [F] 42 C3
St-Vallier-sur-Rhône [F]
　34 B2
St-Vaury [F] 26 A3
St-Véran [F] 34 E4
St-Vincent, Grotte de- [F]
　40 F1
St-Vincent-de-Tyrosse [F]
　30 B4
St. Vincent-du-Lorouèr [F]
　18 C2
St-Vincent-les-Forts [F]
　42 B1
St Vith [B] 14 C2
St-Vivien-de-Médoc [F]
　24 B4
St-Wandrille [F] 10 F2
St-Yan [F] 26 E3
St-Yorre [F] 26 D4
St-Yrieix-la-Perche [F] 24 E4
Sugères [F] 32 E1
Suippes [F] 12 F4
Sully [F] 26 F2
Sully-sur-Loire [F] 18 E3
Surgères [F] 24 C2
Surtainville [F] 10 B1
Survilliers [F] 12 C3
Suscinio, Château de- [F]
　16 C2
Sutrieu [F] 34 D1
Swalmen [NL] 6 C4

T

Tagenac [F] 32 D2
Taillebois [F] 10 D3
Tain-l'Hermitage [F] 34 B3
Taizé [F] 26 F3
Tal ar Groaz [F] 8 B3
Talcy [F] 18 D3
Tallard [F] 34 D4
Talloires [F] 34 E1
Talmont [F] 24 B3
Talmont-St-Hilaire [F] 24 A1
Tancarville [F] 10 E2
Taninges [F] 28 D4
Tanlay [F] 20 C3
Tanus [F] 32 C4
Taponas [F] 26 F4
Tarare [F] 26 E4
Tarascon [F] 40 D2
Tarascon-sur-Ariège [F] 38 C3
Tarbes [F] 36 E3
Tardets-Sorholus [F] 36 C3
Tarnos [F] 30 A4
Tartas [F] 30 B3
Tauves [F] 32 D1
Tavaux [F] 28 B2
Tavernes [F] 40 F3
Tegelen [NL] 6 C3
Teillay [F] 16 E2
Teillet [F] 38 D1
Temse [B] 4 F3
Tence [F] 34 A2
Tende [F] 42 D2
Ter Apel [NL] 2 E3
Tergnier [F] 12 D3

Termes-d'Armagnac [F] 30 D4
Terneuzen [NL] 4 E3
Terrasson-la-Villedieu [F]
　32 B2
Tervuren [B] 4 F4
Tessy-sur-Vire [F] 10 C3
Teysset [F] 30 E3
Thann [F] 22 D4
Tharigné-sur-Duè [F] 18 C2
Thaumiers [F] 26 C2
Thénezay [F] 24 D1
Thenon [F] 30 F1
Théoule [F] 42 C3
Thérouanne [F] 4 C4
Theuley [F] 20 E4
Theux [B] 14 C1
Thevet-St-Julien [F] 26 B2
Theze [F] 36 D2
Thiaucourt-Regniéville [F]
　20 F1
Thiberville [F] 10 E3
Thiélbemont-Farémont [F]
　20 D2
Thiers [F] 26 C4
Thionville [F] 14 C4
Thirette [F] 28 B4
Thivars [F] 18 D1
Thiviers [F] 24 E4
Thizy [F] 26 E4
Thoard [F] 42 B2
Thoissey [F] 26 F4
Thônes [F] 34 E1
Thonon-les-Bains [F] 28
　D4
Thorens-Glières, Château de-
　[F] 34 E1
Thorigné-en-Charnie [F]
　18 A2
Thoronet, Abbaye du- [F]
　40 F3
Thors [F] 20 D2
Thouarcé [F] 16 F3
Thouars [F] 16 F4
Thueyts [F] 32 F3
Thuin [B] 12 F1
Thuir [F] 38 E4
Thuret [F] 26 D4
Thury-Harcourt [F] 10 D3
Tibarrié [F] 38 E1
Tiel [NL] 6 C2
Tielt [B] 4 D4
Tiercé [F] 16 F4
Tignes [F] 34 F2
Tilburg [NL] 6 B3
Til-Châtel [F] 20 E4
Tilloy Lez Mofflaines [F] 12 D1
Tinchebray [F] 10 C3
Tiuccia [F] 44 A3
Tizzano [F] 44 B4
Tombebœuf [F] 30 E3
Tonnay-Boutonne [F] 24 C2
Tonnay-Charente [F] 24 B2
Tonneins [F] 30 E3
Tonnerre [F] 20 C3
Tonquédec, Château de- [F]
　8 C2
Torhout [B] 4 D3
Torigni-sur-Vire [F] 10 C3
Tôtes [F] 12 A2
Toucy [F] 20 B3
Touffou [F] 24 E2
Toul [F] 20 F2
Toulon [F] 40 F4
Toulon sur Allier [F] 26 D3
Toulon-sur-Arroux [F] 26 E2
Toulouse [F] 38 C1
Tourcoing [F] 4 D4
Tourmalet, Col du- [F] 36 E3
Tournan [F] 20 A1
Tournay [F] 36 E3
Tournon [F] 34 B3
Tournon-d'Agenais [F] 30 F3

Tournon-St-Martin [F] 24 F1
Tournus [F] 28 A3
Tourny [F] 12 A3
Tours [F] 18 C3
Tourves [F] 40 F3
Toury [F] 18 E2
Toutes Aures, Col de- [F]
　42 B2
Touvois [F] 16 D3
Trabuc, Grottes de- [F] 40 C1
Trappe d'Aiguebelle, Monastère
　de la- [F] 34 B4
Trappes [F] 12 B4
Travo [F] 44 C3
Tréban [F] 26 D3
Trébeurden [F] 8 C2
Tréboul [F] 8 B3
Trecesson, Château de- [F]
　16 D1
Trégastel [F] 8 C2
Tréguier [F] 8 D2
Treignac [F] 26 A4
Treillieres [F] 16 D2
Trept [F] 34 C1
Trets [F] 40 E3
Tréveray [F] 20 E2
Trévoux [F] 26 F4
Trezelles [F] 26 D3
Triaize [F] 24 B1
Triaucourt-en-Argonne [F]
　20 E1
Trie [F] 36 E3
Trinité, Ermitage de la- [F]
　44 B4
Troarn [F] 10 D3
Trois Fontaines, Abbaye des-
　[F] 20 E2
Trois-Ponts [B] 14 C2
Trôo [F] 18 C2
Trouville [F] 10 E2
Troyes [F] 20 C2
Troyon [F] 20 E1
Truchtersheim [F] 22 E2
Trun [F] 10 D3
Tuchan [F] 38 E3
Tuffé [F] 18 C2
Tulle [F] 32 B1
Tullins [F] 34 C2
Tumulus de Gavrinis [F]
　16 B2
Tuornoel, Château de- [F]
　26 C4
Turckheim [F] 22 D3
Turenne [F] 32 B2
Turnhout [B] 6 B3
Tzummarum [NL] 2 C2

U

Uckange [F] 14 C4
Uddel [NL] 2 C4
Uden [NL] 6 C3
Ugine [F] 34 E1
Uithoorn [NL] 2 B4
Uithuizen [NL] 2 E2
Urbeis [F] 22 D3
Urbise [F] 26 E3
Urçay [F] 26 C2
Urdos [F] 36 D3
Uriage-les-Bains [F]
　34 D3
Urk [NL] 2 C3
Ury [F] 18 F2
Ussé [F] 18 B3
Ussel [F] 32 C1
Usson-du-Poitou [F] 24 E2
Usson-en-Forez [F] 32 F2

Usson–les–Bains [F] 38 D3
Ustaritz [F] 30 A4
Utrecht [NL] 2 B4
Uvernet–Fours [F] 42 B1
Uzel [F] 8 D3
Uzerche [F] 32 B1
Uzès [F] 40 C1
Uzeste [F] 30 D2

Vaas [F] 18 B2
Vaassen [NL] 2 D4
Vabres–l'Abbaye [F] 38 E1
Vaiges [F] 18 A1
Vailly [F] 18 F4
Vaison–la–Romaine [F] 40 D1
Vaite [F] 20 E4
Valberg [F] 42 C2
Valbonnais [F] 34 D3
Val–Claret [F] 34 F2
Valdahon [F] 28 D2
Valderoure [F] 42 BC2
Val d'Esquières [F] 42 B3
Val d'Isère [F] 34 F2
Val–d'Izé [F] 10 B4
Valençay [F] 18 D4
Valence [F] 30 D4
Valence [F] 30 E4
Valence [F] 34 B3
Valence d'Albigeois [F] 32 C4
Valence–sur–Baise [F] 36 F1
Valenciennes [F] 12 E1
Valensole [F] 40 F2
Valentigney [F] 28 E1
Valkenswaard [NL] 6 C3
Valleraugue [F] 40 B1
Vallet [F] 16 E3
Valloire [F] 34 E3
Vallon–en–Sully [F] 26 C2
Vallon–Pont–d'Arc [F] 34 A4
Vallorcine [F] 34 F1
Vallouise [F] 34 E3
Valmigère [F] 38 D3
Valmorel [F] 34 E2
Valognes [F] 10 C1
Valras–Plage [F] 38 F3
Valréas [F] 34 B4
Vals–les–Bains [F] 34 A3
Val–Suzon [F] 28 B1
Val Thorens [F] 34 E3
Vandenesse [F] 26 E2
Vannes [F] 16 C1
Varades [F] 16 E3
Varages [F] 40 F3
Varces [F] 34 D3
Varengeville–sur–Mer [F]
   12 A1
Varennes–en–Argonne [F]
   14 A4
Varilhes [F] 38 C3
Vars [F] 34 E4
Varsseveld [NL] 6 D2
Varzy [F] 20 B4
Vasles [F] 24 D1
Vassy [F] 10 C3
Vatan [F] 18 D4
Vaucelles, Abbaye de– [F]
   12 D2
Vauclaix [F] 26 E1
Vaucluse [F] 28 D2
Vaucouleurs [F] 20 F2
Vaudoy en Brie [F] 20 B1
Vauvenargues [F] 40 E3
Vauvert [F] 40 C2
Vauville [F] 10 B1
Vauvillers [F] 20 F3

Vaux–Le Vicomte [F] 18 F1
Vayrac [F] 32 B2
Veendam [NL] 2 E2
Veenendaal [NL] 6 C2
Veere [NL] 4 E2
Veghel [NL] 6 C3
Veldhoven [NL] 6 B3
Velleclaire [F] 28 C1
Velles [F] 26 A2
Velp [NL] 6 C2
Venaco [F] 44 B2
Vence [F] 42 C3
Vendargues [F] 40 B2
Vendays–Montalivet [F] 24 B4
Vendeuvre [F] 20 D2
Vendôme [F] 18 C2
Vendranges [F] 26 E4
Venlo [NL] 6 D3
Venoy [F] 20 B3
Venray [NL] 6 C3
Ventadour, Château de– [F]
   32 C1
Ventiseri [F] 44 B3
Verberie [F] 12 C3
Verdelles, Château de– [F]
   18 A2
Verdun [F] 14 B4
Verghia [F] 44 A3
Vergt [F] 30 E2
Vermenton [F] 20 B3
Vern–D'anjou [F] 16 F2
Vernet [F] 38 C2
Vernet–les–Bains [F] 38 D4
Verneuil–sur–Avre [F] 10 F4
Vernon [F] 12 A3
Vernoux–en–Gatine [F] 24 C1
Verny [F] 22 C1
Verrières–de–Joux [F] 28 D3
Versailles [F] 12 B4
Versols–et–Lapeyre [F] 38 E1
Verteillac [F] 24 D4
Vertou [F] 16 D3
Vertus [F] 20 C1
Verviers [B] 14 C1
Vervins [F] 12 E2
Verzy [F] 12 E4
Vescovato [F] 44 C2
Vesoul [F] 20 F4
Veules–les–Roses [F] 10 F1
Veulettes–sur–Mer [F] 10 F1
Veurne (Furnes) [B] 4 C3
Veynes [F] 34 D4
Veyrier [F] 34 E1
Vézelay [F] 20 B4
Vézelise [F] 22 C2
Vézénobres [F] 40 C1
Vezin le Coquet [F] 16 D1
Viais [F] 16 D3
Vianden [L] 14 C3
Viane [F] 38 E1
Vianen [NL] 6 B2
Vianne [F] 30 D3
Vias [F] 38 F2
Vibraye [F] 18 C2
Vicdessos [F] 38 C3
Vic–en–Bigorre [F] 36 E2
Vic–Fezensac [F] 30 D4
Vichy [F] 26 D3
Vic–le–Comte [F] 32 E1
Vico [F] 44 A2
Vic–sur–Aisne [F] 12 D3
Vic–sur–Cère [F] 32 D2
Victoire, Abbaye de la– [F]
   12 C3
Vidauban [F] 42 B3
Vielsalm [B] 14 C2
Vienne [F] 34 B2
Vierville [F] 10 C2
Vierzon [F] 18 E4
Vieux–Boucau–les–Bains [F]
   30 A3
Vif [F] 34 D3

Vigneulles [F] 20 F1
Vignory [F] 20 E2
Vihiers [F] 16 F3
Village, Roche aux– [F] 14 A2
Villagrains [F] 30 C2
Villaines la Gonais [F] 18 C2
Villaines–la–Juhel [F] 10 D4
Villandraut [F] 30 C2
Villandry [F] 18 B3
Villard–de–Lans [F] 34 C3
Villardebelle [F] 38 D3
Villars–les–Dombes [F] 28 A4
Villars–sur–Var [F] 42 C2
Villé [F] 22 D3
Villebois–Lavalette [F] 24 D4
Ville–Devant–Chaumont [F]
   14 B4
Villedieu–les–Poêles [F] 10 C3
Villédomain [F] 18 C4
Ville–en–Tardenois [F] 12 E4
Villefagnan [F] 24 D3
Villefontaine [F] 34 C2
Villefort [F] 32 F4
Villefranche [F] 42 C3
Villefranche–d'Albigeois [F]
   38 D1
Villefranche–de–Conflent [F]
   38 D4
Villefranche–de–Lauragais [F]
   38 C2
Villefranche–de–Lonchat [F]
   30 D2
Villefranche–de–Panat [F] 32 C4
Villefranche–de–Rouergue [F]
   32 B3
Villefranche–du–Périgord [F]
   30 F3
Villefranche–sur–Cher [F] 18 D4
Villefranche–sur–Saône [F]
   26 F4
Villegats [F] 24 D3
Villemur [F] 32 A4
Villenauxe–la–Grande [F] 20 C1
Villeneuve [F] 32 C3
Villeneuve [F] 40 D2
Villeneuve–de–Berg [F] 34 B4
Villeneuve–de–Marsan [F]
   30 C4
Villeneuve–l'Archevêque [F]
   20 B2
Villeneuve–Loubet [F] 42 C3
Villeneuve–sur–Allier [F] 26 D2
Villeneuve–sur–Lot [F] 30 E3
Villeneuve–sur–Yonne [F] 20 B2
Villerbon [F] 18 D3
Villeréal [F] 30 E3
Villeromain [F] 18 D3
Villers [B] 14 A1
Villers [F] 10 E2
Villers–Bocage [F] 10 D3
Villers–Bretonneux [F] 12 C2
Villers–Cotterêts [F] 12 D3
Villersexel [F] 28 D1
Villers–le–Lac [F] 28 D2
Villerville [F] 10 E2
Villeseque [F] 30 F3
Ville–sur–Illon [F] 22 C3
Villiers–St–Georges [F] 20 B1
Villon [F] 20 C3
Vimoutiers [F] 10 E3
Vinay [F] 34 C2
Vinça [F] 38 D4
Vingrau [F] 38 E3
Vinon–sur–Verdon [F] 40 F2
Violès [F] 40 D1
Vire [F] 10 C3
Viré [F] 28 A3
Vire Court [F] 8 B4
Virieu [F] 34 C2
Virieu–le–Grand [F] 34 D1
Vironvay [F] 12 A3
Virton [B] 14 B3

Visé [B] 14 C1
Vitré [F] 16 E1
Vitry–le–François [F] 20 D1
Vitteaux [F] 20 C4
Vittel [F] 20 F3
Vivario [F] 44 B2
Vivier, Château du– [F]
   20 A1
Viviers [F] 34 B4
Vivonne [F] 24 D2
Vizille [F] 34 D3
Vizzavona [F] 44 B3
Vlaardingen [NL] 4 F2
Vlagtweed [NL] 2 E3
Vlieland [NL] 2 C2
Vlissingen [NL] 4 E3
Void [F] 20 F2
Voiron [F] 34 D2
Voise [F] 18 E1
Voix [F] 40 F2
Volendam [NL] 2 B3
Vollenhove [NL] 2 D3
Volvic [F] 26 C4
Voneche [B] 14 A2
Voorschoten [NL] 2 A4
Voorst [NL] 2 D4
Voreppe [F] 34 D2
Vorey [F] 32 F2
Vouillé [F] 24 D1
Voulpaix [F] 12 E2
Voulx [F] 20 AB2
Vouvant [F] 24 C1
Vouvray [F] 18 C3
Voves [F] 18 D2
Vresse [B] 14 A2
Vriezenveen [NL] 2 E4
Vrigny [F] 12 E4
Vroomshoop [NL] 2 D4
Vroville [F] 22 C3
Vry [F] 14 C4
Vue [F] 16 D3
Vught [NL] 6 B3

Waalwijk [NL] 6 B2
Wageningen [NL] 6 C2
Walcourt [B] 12 F2
Waldenbourg [F] 22 D2
Waregem [B] 4 D4
Waremme [B] 14 B1
Warnsveld [NL] 6 D2
Wasigenstein, Château de– [F]
   22 E1
Wasselonne [F] 22 E2
Wassenaar [NL] 2 A4
Wasserbillig [L] 14 C3
Wassy [F] 20 E2
Watten [F] 4 C4
Waulsort [B] 14 A2
Weert [NL] 6 C3
Well [NL] 6 C3
Wellin [B] 14 B2
Wemperhaardt [L] 14 C2
Wépion [B] 14 A1
Werbomont [B] 14 C2
Westende–Bad [B] 4 D3
Westerlo [B] 6 B4
Westkapelle [NL] 4 E2
West–Terschelling [NL] 2 C1
Wetteren [B] 4 E4
Wierden [NL] 2 D4
Wijhe [NL] 2 D4
Willebroek [B] 4 F4
Willemstad [NL] 4 F2
Wilsin [NL] 2 B4
Wiltz [L] 14 C2

Wimereux [F] 4 B4
Wingen–sur–Moder [F] 22 D2
Winschoten [NL] 2 E2
Winsum [NL] 2 E2
Winterswijk [NL] 6 E2
Wissant [F] 4 B3
Wissembourg [F] 22 E1
Woerden [NL] 2 B4
Woerth [F] 22 E2
Woesten [B] 4 D4
Wolvega [NL] 2 D3
Workum [NL] 2 C2
Wormerveer [NL] 2 B3
Wormhout [F] 4 C4
Wuustwezel [B] 6 A3

Xertigny [F] 22 C3
Xhoffraix [B] 14 C1

Ychoux [F] 30 B2
Yenne [F] 34 D2
Yerville [F] 10 F2
Yport [F] 10 E2
Ypres (Ieper) [B] 4 D4
Yquem, Château– [F] 30 D2
Yrouerre [F] 20 C3
Yssandon, Puy d'– [F]
   32 B1
Yssingeaux [F] 32 F2
Yvetot [F] 10 F2
Yvoir [B] 14 A1
Yvoire [F] 28 C4

Zaandam [NL] 2 B3
Zaltbommel [NL] 6 B2
Zandhoven [B] 4 F3
Zandvoort [NL] 2 B3
Zeebrugge [B] 4 D3
Zeewolde [NL] 2 C4
Zeist [NL] 2 C4
Zelhem [NL] 6 D2
Zelzate [B] 4 E3
Zevenaar [NL] 6 D2
Zevenergen [NL] 6 A2
Zicavo [F] 44 B3
Zierikzee [NL] 4 E2
Zijpe [NL] 4 F2
Zoetermeer [NL] 2 A4
Zoeterwoude [NL] 2 A4
Zolder [B] 6 B4
Zonhoven [B] 6 B4
Zonza [F] 44 B3
Zoutkamp [NL] 2 D2
Zoutleeuw [B] 6 B4
Zuani [F] 44 C2
Zuidhorn [NL] 2 D2
Zuidlaren [NL] 2 E2
Zundert [NL] 6 A3
Zutphen [NL] 6 D2
Zwijndrecht [NL] 6 B2
Zwolle [NL] 2 D3

CHARLIE PARKER OMNIBOOK

For E♭ Instruments • Transcribed Exactly from His Recorded Solos

Transcribed by Chris Stewart

Cover art based on photo from Getty Images/William Gottlieb / Contributor

ISBN 978-1-5400-2196-0

HAL•LEONARD®

Visit Hal Leonard Online at
www.halleonard.com

Contact us:
Hal Leonard
7777 West Bluemound Road
Milwaukee, WI 53213
Email: info@halleonard.com

In Europe, contact:
Hal Leonard Europe Limited
42 Wigmore Street
Marylebone, London, W1U 2RN
Email: info@halleonardeurope.com

In Australia, contact:
Hal Leonard Australia Pty. Ltd.
4 Lentara Court
Cheltenham, Victoria, 3192 Australia
Email: info@halleonard.com.au

PREFACE

The **Charlie Parker Omnibook** was life changing for many of us when first released by Jamey Aebersold and Ken Slone in 1978. Before that, most jazz musicians listened to their LPs over and over until the vinyl was destroyed. If you loved a particular lick, you repeatedly lifted up the phono arm and dropped it back to hear it again and again.

Someone figured out that if you recorded the LP on a cassette at high speed, you could slow the solo to half speed when played back on a normal speed player. Bird now sounded exactly like a bari sax player, an octave lower. You could hear difficult licks more easily this way. Also, it was a great method to preserve your vinyl records! That was how my generation learned jazz. With the analog cassette tape method I transcribed almost all Cannonball Adderley's music and penned them by hand. Similarly, the Omnibook is a collection of transcriptions created with these original analog techniques and penned by hand calligraphy.

Then digital technology became available to anyone with a home computer. Now you could play a recording at any tempo, tune it, and then equalize it to focus on the instrument of interest. I went through my prior transcriptions and was amazed at how many things I transcribed "wrong" simply due to lack of discernment using the analog technique. I would never go back to my old ways after that discovery.

Digital transcribing was revolutionary and even created a whole new art form. If you transcribed a solo "perfectly" at a slow tempo, it didn't sound quite right at the original tempo. Appreciating this phenomenon and knowing when to settle with a certain note, riff or rhythm became the new art of jazz solo transcription. Computers can never replace a human's discernment. Music engraving software exploded to the point of making hand engraving or calligraphy obsolete. None of this existed when the Omnibook was first released.

So doesn't it follow to re-do the original Omnibook? I took on the challenge of creating a *Charlie Parker Omnibook in the new digital era*. I approached the project like an academician who wanted to correct all the errors and release a more accurate second edition. Well, if transcribing is considered an art form, then what is the consequence of redoing classic art?

Hal Leonard Publishing expressed that the original Charlie Parker Omnibook was a classic and should be allowed to remain the special work that it is. It represents what was going on in jazz, education, and technology during the pre-digital era. But as a jazz saxophonist, transcriptionist, and academician, I just want the right notes! The common ground between art, technology, and wanting the right notes was to publish an entirely different second volume with sixty new solos. This book is the result of that happy compromise.

There are a few differences between the two Omnibook volumes worth mentioning. Two titles have been repeated from the original book including Confirmation and Visa. The first represents one of Bird's biggest hits played in an entirely different fashion from the version in the original Omnibook and is one of his most outstanding solo performances of all time. Transcribing the alternate Birdland version of Visa showcases my skillful use of technology to resurrect a solo that is incomplete and nearly inaudible. I've included more ballad performances that are a must for any jazz alto player to know. You will also appreciate some teenage Bird when you discover the obvious genius of what was to come from some early recordings. The original Omnibook also contains sixty tunes, but all were written by Charlie Parker. I have included many tunes by other authors in this volume. This permitted the last difference where I made an effort to include titles where we discover Bird approaching tunes with more complex chord changes and less common key signatures. The original Omnibook clearly is a speed demon with several tunes exceeding 360 bpm (6 beats/sec.) - although this volume still has several burners exceeding 300 bpm that will challenge the most adept player. You can then cool off with some ballads.

What you're about to experience comes from thousands of hours of analysis and collaboration, and my love of jazz music, all tuned toward carrying on the legacy of the original Charlie Parker Omnibook in a new digital era. It is my hope that it continues to be a major reference for students of jazz, professional musicians and music historians for years to come.

Chris "Doc" Stewart, M.D., F.A.C.E.P.
Senior Consultant & Assistant Professor
Mayo Clinic School of Medicine

4	BIRD FEATHERS	112	LIZA (ALL THE CLOUDS'LL ROLL AWAY)
6	BIRD OF PARADISE	124	LOVE FOR SALE
9	BIRD'S NEST	128	LOVER
12	BODY AND SOUL	119	MANGO MANGUE
16	BONGO BEEP	132	MEANDERING
18	BONGO BOP	134	MOVE
20	CARVIN' THE BIRD	142	MY HEART BELONGS TO DADDY
22	CHEERS	145	MY HEART TELLS ME
25	CHEROKEE (INDIAN LOVE SONG)	148	MY OLD FLAME
30	CONFIRMATION	151	A NIGHT IN TUNISIA
38	COOL BLUES	156	OH, LADY BE GOOD!
44	CRAZEOLOGY	158	ON A SLOW BOAT TO CHINA
46	DEXTERITY	161	OUT OF NOWHERE
35	DIZZY ATMOSPHERE	164	QUASIMODO
48	DRIFTING ON A REED	166	REPETITION
50	EAST OF THE SUN (AND WEST OF THE MOON)	169	ROCK SALT a/k/a ROCKER
56	EASY TO LOVE (YOU'D BE SO EASY TO LOVE)	176	'ROUND MIDNIGHT
		178	SALT PEANUTS
53	EMBRACEABLE YOU	182	SIPPIN' AT BELLS
60	GROOVIN' HIGH	184	THE SONG IS YOU
68	HALLELUJAH	188	THE SQUIRREL
70	HOT HOUSE	195	STAR EYES
74	I GET A KICK OUT OF YOU	198	STUPENDOUS
78	I REMEMBER YOU	200	SWEDISH SCHNAPPS
82	I'LL REMEMBER APRIL	202	SWEET GEORGIA BROWN
90	I'VE FOUND A NEW BABY (I FOUND A NEW BABY)	206	THEY DIDN'T BELIEVE ME
		224	THIS TIME THE DREAM'S ON ME
94	I'VE GOT YOU UNDER MY SKIN	210	TINY'S TEMPO
98	INDIANA (BACK HOME AGAIN IN INDIANA)	212	VISA
		216	WEE (ALLEN'S ALLEY)
65	KLACTOVEEDEDSTENE	220	WHAT IS THIS THING CALLED LOVE?
106	LITTLE WILLIE LEAPS		

Bird Feathers

Recorded November 4, 1947 *A Studio Chronicle 1940-1948* (JSP Records JSP915)
By Charlie Parker

Bird of Paradise

Recorded October 28, 1947 *A Studio Chronicle 1940-1948* (JSP Records JSP915)
By Charlie Parker

Bird's Nest

Recorded February 19, 1947 *A Studio Chronicle 1940-1948* (JSP Records JSP915)
By Charlie Parker

10

Body and Soul

Recorded February 19, 1941 *Charlie Parker: A Studio Chronicle* (JSP Records JSP915A)
Words by Edward Heyman, Robert Sour and Frank Eyton
Music by Johnny Green

14

Bongo Beep

Recorded December 17, 1947 *A Studio Chronicle 1940-1948* (JSP Records JSP915)
By Charlie Parker

17

Bongo Bop

Recorded February 19, 1947 *A Studio Chronicle 1940-1948* (JSP Records JSP915)
By Charlie Parker

Carvin' the Bird

Recorded February 19, 1947 *A Studio Chronicle 1940-1948* (JSP Records JSP915)
By Charlie Parker

Cheers

Recorded February 26, 1947 *A Studio Chronicle 1940-1948* (JSP Records JSP915)
By Howard McGhee

Cherokee (Indian Love Song)

Recorded September, 1941 *Charlie Parker: A Studio Chronicle* (JSP Records JSP915a)
Words and Music by Ray Noble

Confirmation

Recorded September 29, 1947 *The Complete Carnegie Hall Performances* (Definitive DRCD 11375_4)
By Charlie Parker

31

33

34

Dizzy Atmosphere

Recorded February 28, 1945 *A Studio Chronicle 1940-1948* (JSP Records JSP915)
By John "Dizzy" Gillespie

Cool Blues

Recorded March 8, 1953 *Charlie Parker - The Washington Concerts* (Blue Note 7243 5 22626 2 5)
By Charlie Parker

Crazeology

Recorded December 1, 1947 *Boss Bird: Studio Recordings 1944-1951* (Proper Box B000069DWX)
By Benny Harris

Dexterity

Recorded October 28, 1947 *A Studio Chronicle 1940-1948* (JSP Records JSP915)
By Charlie Parker

Drifting on a Reed

Recorded December 17, 1947 *A Studio Chronicle 1940-1948* (JSP Records JSP915)
By Charlie Parker

49

East of the Sun (And West of the Moon)

Recorded August 31, 1950 *The Complete Verve Master Takes* (Verve LC 00383)
Words and Music by Brooks Bowman

Embraceable You

Recorded October 28, 1947 *A Studio Chronicle 1940-1948* (JSP Records JSP915)
Music and Lyrics by George Gershwin and Ira Gershwin

Easy to Love (You'd Be So Easy to Love)

Recorded June 1950 *Complete Live at Cafe Society* (Rare Live Recordings RLR 88635)
Words and Music by Cole Porter

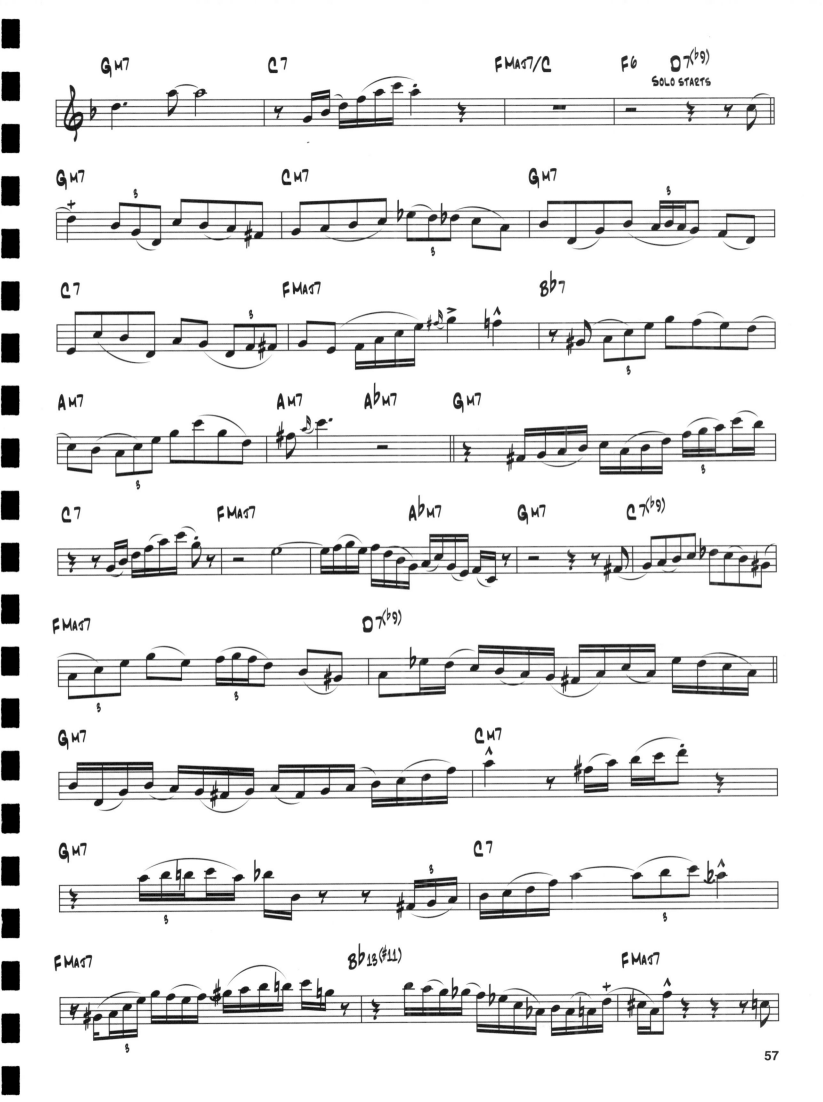

57

Groovin' High

Recorded September 29, 1947 *The Complete Carnegie Hall Performances* (Definitive DRCD 11375_4)
By John "Dizzy" Gillespie

63

Klactoveededstene

Recorded November 4, 1947 *A Studio Chronicle 1940-1948* (JSP Records JSP915)
By Charlie Parker

Hallelujah

Recorded May 11, 1945 *A Studio Chronicle 1940-1948* (JSP Records JSP915)
Words and Music by Clifford Grey, Leo Robin and Vincent Youmans

Hot House

Recorded January 15, 1949 *The Complete Live Performances on Savoy* (Savoy SVY-17021-24)
By Tadd Dameron

I Get a Kick Out of You

Recorded March 31, 1954 *Bird: The Complete Charlie Parker on Verve* (Verve 837 143-2)
Words and Music by Cole Porter

I Remember You

Recorded July 30, 1953 *The Complete Verve Master Takes* (Verve LC 00383)
Words by Johnny Mercer
Music by Victor Schertzinger

I'll Remember April

Recorded April 12, 1951 *Charlie Parker – The Happy "Bird"* (Collectables CDL-5787)
Words and Music by Pat Johnston, Don Raye and Gene De Paul

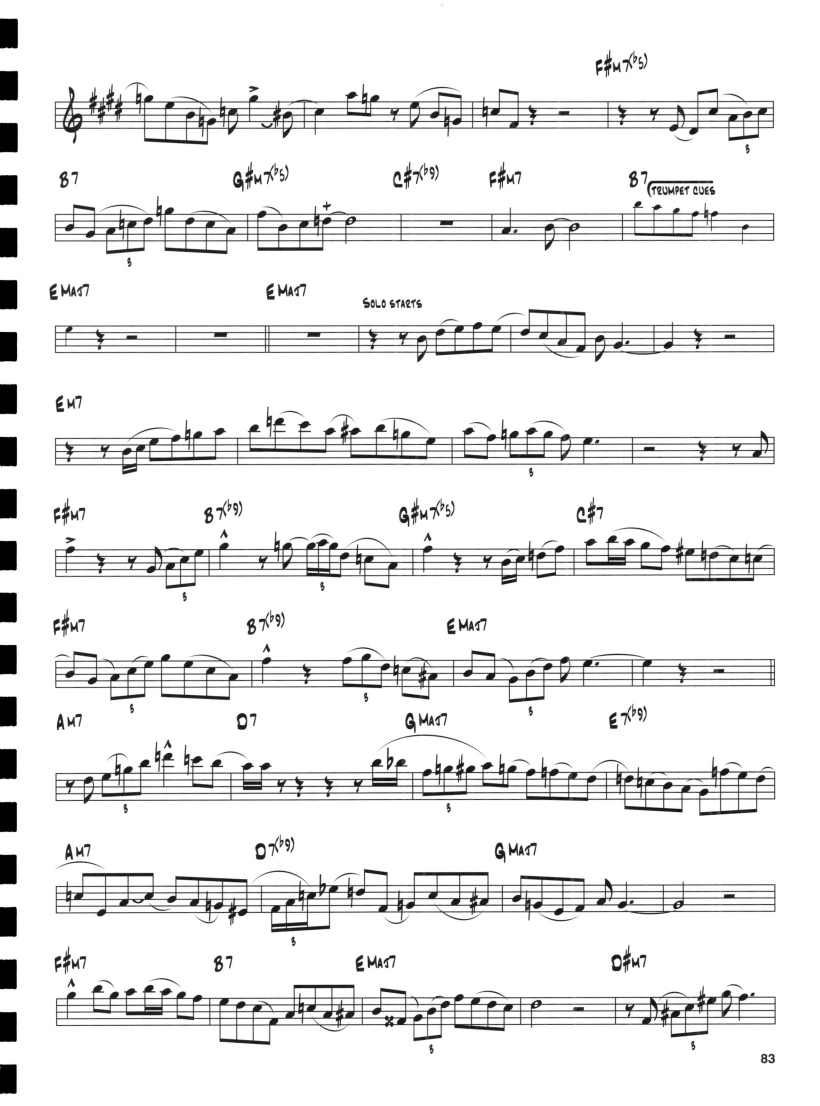

I've Found a New Baby (I Found a New Baby)

Recorded September, 1941 *Charlie Parker: A Studio Chronicle* (JSP Records JSP915A)
Words and Music by Jack Palmer and Spencer Williams

92

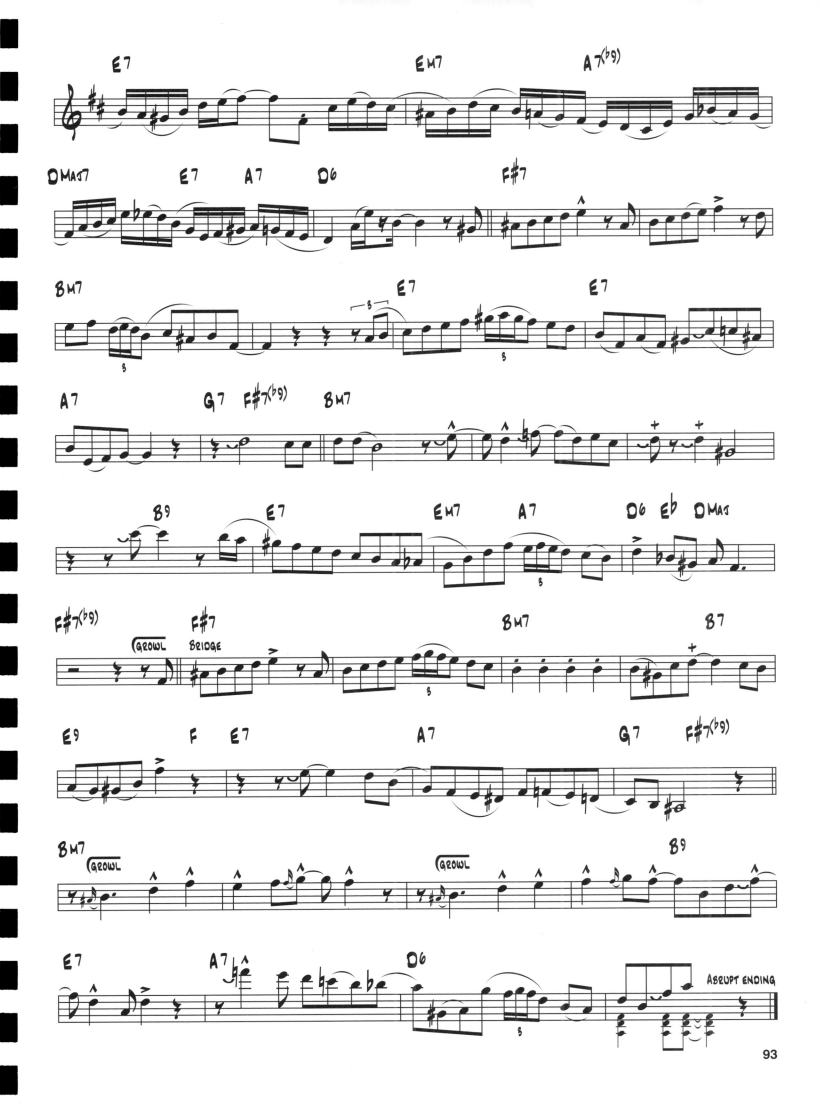

I've Got You Under My Skin

Recorded March 31, 1954 *The Complete Verve Master Takes* (Verve LC 00383)
Words and Music by Cole Porter

97

Indiana (Back Home Again in Indiana)

Recorded June 6, 1952 *Complete Jam Sessions* (Definitive Records DRCD 11231)
Words by Ballard MacDonald
Music by James F. Hanley

Little Willie Leaps

Recorded May 15, 1950 *Charlie Parker at Birdland, Vol. 1* (TKO Records FBB 901/2)
By Miles Davis

111

Liza (All the Clouds'll Roll Away)

Recorded June 16, 1952 *Complete Jam Sessions* (Definitive Records DRCD 11231)
Music by George Gershwin
Lyrics by Ira Gershwin and Gus Kahn

Mango Mangue

Recorded December 20, 1948 *A Studio Chronicle 1940-1948* (JSP Records JSP915)
Words and Music by Marion Sunshine and Gilbert Valdez

Love for Sale

Recorded December 10, 1954 *Bird: The Complete Charlie Parker on Verve* (Verve 837 143-2)
Words and Music by Cole Porter

127

Lover

Recorded January 22, 1952 *The Complete Verve Master Takes* (Verve LC 00383)
Words by Lorenz Hart
Music by Richard Rodgers

129

Meandering

Recorded Noverber 26, 1945 *A Studio Chronicle 1940-1948* (JSP Records JSP915)
By Charlie Parker

Move

Recorded May 15, 1950 *Charlie Parker at Birdland* (TKO Records FBB 901/2)
By Denzil De Costa Best

139

w/Trumpet (Parker bottom 2nd x only)

Parker

AD LIB

141

My Heart Belongs to Daddy

Recorded March 31, 1954 *Bird: The Complete Charlie Parker on Verve* (Verve 837 143-2)
Words and Music by Cole Porter

143

My Heart Tells Me

Recorded September, 1941 *Charlie Parker: A Studio Chronicle 1940-1948* (JSP Records JSP915)
Words by Mack Gordon
Music by Harry Warren

146

My Old Flame

Recorded November 4, 1947 *A Studio Chronicle 1940-1948* (JSP Records JSP915)
Words and Music by Aurthur Johnston and Sam Coslow

A Night in Tunisia

Recorded September 29, 1947 *The Complete Carnegie Hall Performances* (Definitive DRCD 11375_4)
By John "Dizzy" Gillespie and Frank Paparelli

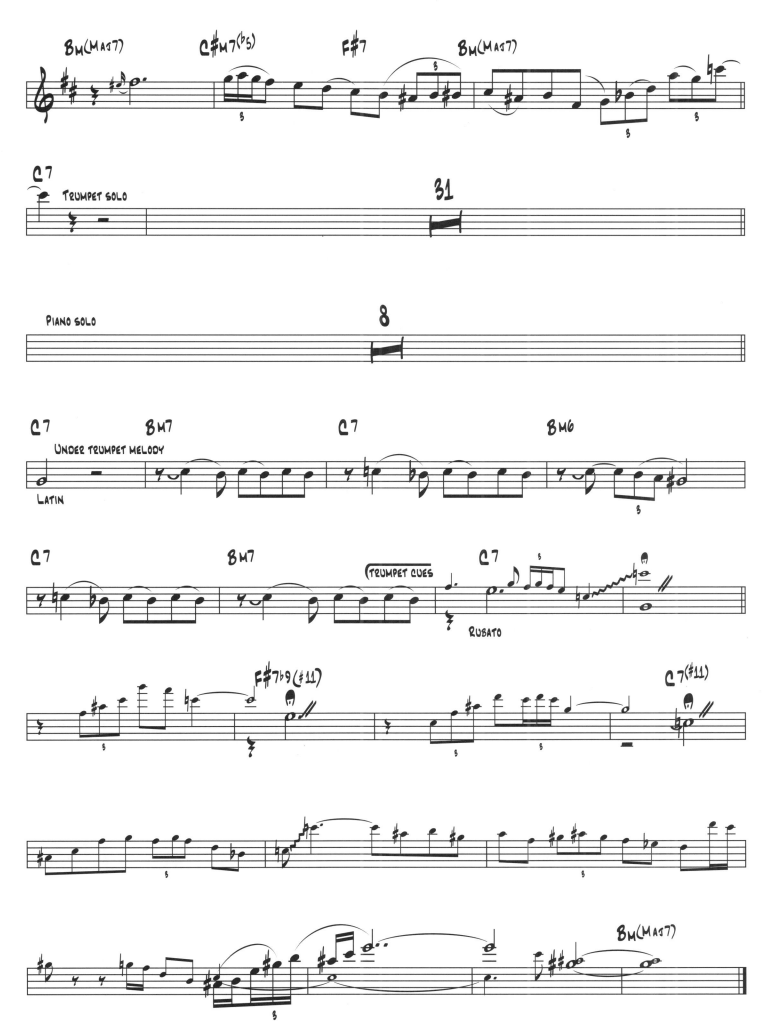

Oh, Lady Be Good!

Recorded December 3, 1940 *A Studio Chronicle 1940-1948* (JSP Records JSP915)
Music and Lyrics by George Gershwin and Ira Gershwin

On a Slow Boat to China

Recorded March 12, 1949 *Newly Discovered Sides by Charlie Parker* (Savoy Jazz SV-0156)
By Frank Loesser

159

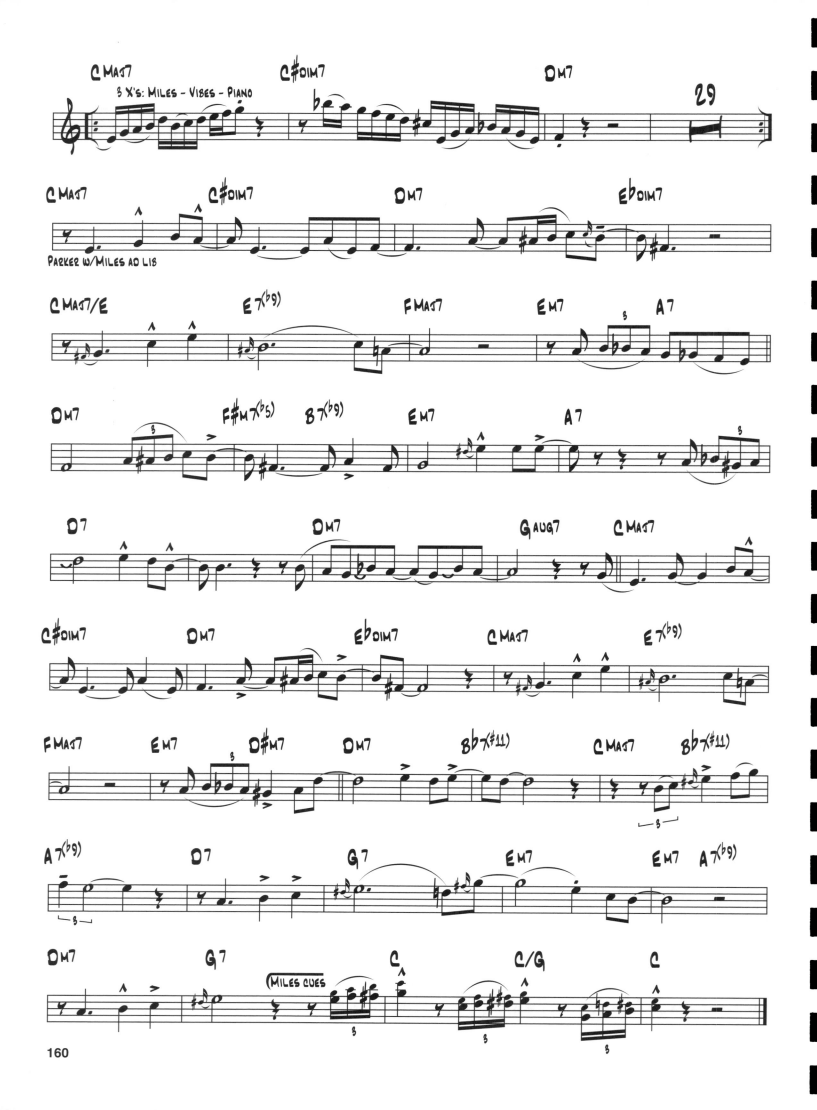

Out of Nowhere

Recorded March 10, 1953 *Complete Storyville Performances* (Jazz Factory JFCD 22876)
Words by Edward Heyman
Music by Johnny Green

162

Quasimodo

Recorded December 17, 1947 *A Studio Chronicle 1940-1948* (JSP Records JSP915)
By Charlie Parker

Repetition

Recorded September 17, 1950 *Bird: The Complete Charlie Parker on Verve* (Verve 837 143-2)
By Neil Hefti

Rock Salt a/k/a Rocker

Recorded September 26, 1952 *Complete Live at the Rockland Palace* (Rare Live Recordings RLR 88641)
By Gerry Mulligan

174

'Round Midnight

Recorded March 31, 1951 *Charlie Parker at Birdland* (TKO Records FBB 901/2)
Music by Thelonious Monk and Cootie Williams
Words by Bernie Hanighen

Salt Peanuts

Recorded December 1950 *Complete Live at the Rockland Palace* (Rare Live Recordings RLR 88641)
By John "Dizzy" Gillespie and Kenny Clarke

Sippin' at Bells

Recorded September 13, 1947 *A Studio Chronicle 1940-1948* (JSP Records JSP915)
By Miles Davis

The Song Is You

Recorded December 1952 *The Complete Verve Master Takes* (Verve LC 00383)
Lyrics by Oscar Hammerstein II
Music by Jerome Kern

The Squirrel

Recorded June 16, 1952 *Complete Jam Sessions* (Definitive Records DRCD 11231)
By Tadd Dameron

194

Star Eyes

Recorded March or April 1950 *The Complete Verve Master Takes* (Verve LC 00383)
Words by Don Raye
Music by Gene De Paul

Stupendous

Recorded February 26, 1947 *A Studio Chronicle 1940-1948* (JSP Records JSP915)
By Howard McGhee

199

Swedish Schnapps

Recorded August 8, 1951 *Bird: The Complete Charlie Parker on Verve* (Verve 837 143-2)
By Charlie Shavers

Sweet Georgia Brown

Recorded January 28, 1946 *Bird: The Complete Charlie Parker on Verve* (Verve 837 143-2)
Words and Music by Ben Bernie, Maceo Pinkard and Kenneth Casey

14 X's: Tenor 3 - Dizzy 3 - Alto 2 - Tenor 3 - Trumpet 3

31

They Didn't Believe Me

Recorded June 16, 1952 *Complete Jam Sessions* (Definitive Records DRCD 11231)
Words by Herbert Reynolds
Music by Jerome Kern

Tiny's Tempo

Recorded December 15, 1945 *A Studio Chronicle 1940-1948* (JSP Records JSP915)
By Clyde Hart and Lloyd Grimes

Visa

Recorded February 14, 1950 *Charlie Parker at Birdland, Vol. 1* **(TKO Records FBB 901/1)**
By Charlie Parker

Wee (Allen's Alley)

Recorded May 15, 1953 *Complete Jazz at Massey Hall* (Jazz Factory JFCD 22856)
By Denzil DeCosta Best

What Is This Thing Called Love?

Recorded June 1952 *Bird: The Complete Charlie Parker on Verve* (Verve 837 143-2)
Words and Music by Cole Porter

This Time the Dream's on Me

Recorded September 26, 1952 *Complete Live at the Rockland Palace* (Rare Live Recordings RLR 88641)
Words by Johnny Mercer
Music by Harold Arlen

228

THE REAL BOOK MULTI-TRACKS

TODAY'S BEST WAY TO PRACTICE JAZZ!
Accurate, easy-to-read lead sheets and professional, customizable audio tracks accessed online for 10 songs.

1. MAIDEN VOYAGE PLAY-ALONG
Autumn Leaves • Blue Bossa • Doxy • Footprints • Maiden Voyage • Now's the Time • On Green Dolphin Street • Satin Doll • Summertime • Tune Up.
00196616 Book with Online Media..$17.99

2. MILES DAVIS PLAY-ALONG
Blue in Green • Boplicity (Be Bop Lives) • Four • Freddie Freeloader • Milestones • Nardis • Seven Steps to Heaven • So What • Solar • Walkin'.
00196798 Book with Online Media..$17.99

3. ALL BLUES PLAY-ALONG
All Blues • Back at the Chicken Shack • Billie's Bounce (Bill's Bounce) • Birk's Works • Blues by Five • C-Jam Blues • Mr. P.C. • One for Daddy-O • Reunion Blues • Turnaround.
00196692 Book with Online Media..$17.99

4. CHARLIE PARKER PLAY-ALONG
Anthropology • Blues for Alice • Confirmation • Donna Lee • K.C. Blues • Moose the Mooche • My Little Suede Shoes • Ornithology • Scrapple from the Apple • Yardbird Suite.
00196799 Book with Online Media..$17.99

5. JAZZ FUNK PLAY-ALONG
Alligator Bogaloo • The Chicken • Cissy Strut • Cold Duck Time • Comin' Home Baby • Mercy, Mercy, Mercy • Put It Where You Want It • Sidewinder • Tom Cat • Watermelon Man.
00196728 Book with Online Media..$17.99

6. SONNY ROLLINS PLAY-ALONG
Airegin • Blue Seven • Doxy • Duke of Iron • Oleo • Pent up House • St. Thomas • Sonnymoon for Two • Strode Rode • Tenor Madness.
00218264 Book with Online Media..$17.99

7. THELONIOUS MONK PLAY-ALONG
Bemsha Swing • Blue Monk • Bright Mississippi • Green Chimneys • Monk's Dream • Reflections • Rhythm-a-ning • 'Round Midnight • Straight No Chaser • Ugly Beauty.
00232768 Book with Online Media..$17.99

8. BEBOP ERA PLAY-ALONG
Au Privave • Boneology • Bouncing with Bud • Dexterity • Groovin' High • Half Nelson • In Walked Bud • Lady Bird • Move • Witches Pit.
00196728 Book with Online Media..$17.99

9. CHRISTMAS CLASSICS PLAY-ALONG
Blue Christmas • Christmas Time Is Here • Frosty the Snow Man • Have Yourself a Merry Little Christmas • I'll Be Home for Christmas • My Favorite Things • Santa Claus Is Comin' to Town • Silver Bells • White Christmas • Winter Wonderland.
00236808 Book with Online Media..$17.99

10. CHRISTMAS SONGS PLAY-ALONG
Away in a Manger • The First Noel • Go, Tell It on the Mountain • Hark! the Herald Angels Sing • Jingle Bells • Joy to the World • O Come, All Ye Faithful • O Holy Night • Up on the Housetop • We Wish You a Merry Christmas.
00236809 Book with Online Media..$17.99

15. CHRISTMAS TUNES PLAY-ALONG
The Christmas Song (Chestnuts Roasting on an Open Fire) • Do You Hear What I Hear • Feliz Navidad • Here Comes Santa Claus (Right down Santa Claus Lane) • A Holly Jolly Christmas • Let It Snow! Let It Snow! Let It Snow! • The Little Drummer Boy • The Most Wonderful Time of the Year • Rudolph the Red-Nosed Reindeer • Sleigh Ride.
00278073 Book with Online Media..$17.99

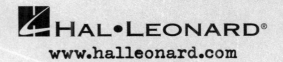

HAL•LEONARD®
www.halleonard.com

Prices, content and availability subject to change without notice.

0718

HAL•LEONARD SAXOPHONE PLAY-ALONG

The *Saxophone Play-Along Series* will help you play your favorite songs quickly and easily. Just follow the music, listen to the audio to hear how the saxophone should sound, and then play along using the separate backing tracks. Each song is printed twice in the book: once for alto and once for tenor saxes. The online audio is available for streaming or download using the unique code printed inside the book, and it includes **PLAYBACK+** options such as looping and tempo adjustments.

1. ROCK 'N' ROLL
Bony Moronie • Charlie Brown • Hand Clappin' • Honky Tonk (Parts 1 & 2) • I'm Walkin' • Lucille (You Won't Do Your Daddy's Will) • See You Later, Alligator • Shake, Rattle and Roll.
00113137 Book/Online Audio $16.99

2. R&B
Cleo's Mood • I Got a Woman • Pick up the Pieces • Respect • Shot Gun • Soul Finger • Soul Serenade • Unchain My Heart.
00113177 Book/Online Audio $16.99

3. CLASSIC ROCK
Baker Street • Deacon Blues • The Heart of Rock and Roll • Jazzman • Smooth Operator • Turn the Page • Who Can It Be Now? • Young Americans.
00113429 Book/Online Audio $16.99

4. SAX CLASSICS
Boulevard of Broken Dreams • Harlem Nocturne • Night Train • Peter Gunn • The Pink Panther • St. Thomas • Tequila • Yakety Sax.
00114393 Book/Online Audio. $16.99

5. CHARLIE PARKER
Billie's Bounce (Bill's Bounce) • Confirmation • Dewey Square • Donna Lee • Now's the Time • Ornithology • Scrapple from the Apple • Yardbird Suite.
00118286 Book/Online Audio $16.99

6. DAVE KOZ
All I See Is You • Can't Let You Go (The Sha La Song) • Emily • Honey-Dipped • Know You by Heart • Put the Top Down • Together Again • You Make Me Smile.
00118292 Book/Online Audio $16.99

7. GROVER WASHINGTON, JR.
East River Drive • Just the Two of Us • Let It Flow • Make Me a Memory (Sad Samba) • Mr. Magic • Take Five • Take Me There • Winelight.
00118293 Book/Online Audio $16.99

8. DAVID SANBORN
Anything You Want • Bang Bang • Chicago Song • Comin' Home Baby • The Dream • Hideaway • Slam • Straight to the Heart.
00125694 Book/Online Audio $16.99

9. CHRISTMAS
The Christmas Song (Chestnuts Roasting on an Open Fire) • Christmas Time Is Here • Count Your Blessings Instead of Sheep • Do You Hear What I Hear • Have Yourself a Merry Little Christmas • The Little Drummer Boy • White Christmas • Winter Wonderland.
00148170 Book/Online Audio $16.99

10. JOHN COLTRANE
Blue Train (Blue Trane) • Body and Soul • Central Park West • Cousin Mary • Giant Steps • Like Sonny (Simple Like) • My Favorite Things • Naima (Niema).
00193333 Book/Online Audio $16.99

11. JAZZ ICONS
Body and Soul • Con Alma • Oleo • Speak No Evil • Take Five • There Will Never Be Another You • Tune Up • Work Song.
00199296 Book/Online Audio $16.99

12. SMOOTH JAZZ
Bermuda Nights • Blue Water • Europa • Flirt • Love Is on the Way • Maputo • Songbird • Winelight.
00248670 Book/Online Audio $16.99

13. BONEY JAMES
Butter • Let It Go • Stone Groove • Stop, Look, Listen (To Your Heart) • Sweet Thing • Tick Tock • Total Experience • Vinyl.
00257186 Book/Online Audio $16.99

Visit Hal Leonard online at **www.halleonard.com**